World Tourism Organization

Market Intelligence and Promotion Section

Sustainable Development of Tourism Section

Madrid, January 2002

The U.S.
Ecotourism Market

Special Report, Number 12

Capitán Haya 42
28020 Madrid
Tel: (34) 91 567 81 00
Fax: (34) 91 571 37 33
E-mail: omt@world-tourism.org
Internet: www.world-tourism.org

The U.S. Ecotourism Market

ISBN: 92-844-0490-8

Published by the World Tourism Organization
Madrid, Spain

Printed by the World Tourism Organization. Madrid, Spain

Foreword

Background

In view of the sustained growth of tourism activity worldwide, it would be reasonable to assume that the ecotourism sector will develop along parallel lines. However, no extensive international market research has hitherto been conducted with a view to corroborating this hypothesis.

On the occasion of the designation by the United Nations of 2002 as the International Year of Ecotourism (IYE), the World Tourism Organization (WTO) has decided to undertake research with a view to increasing knowledge of the following seven countries in their capacity as ecotourism generating markets: Germany, USA, United Kingdom, Canada, Spain, France and Italy[1].

Market studies of this type must be based on a coordinated approach among the experts concerned, similar research methods and, more importantly, a common concept of the term «ecotourism» if they are to deliver well-founded conclusions and global recommendations. However, concepts of ecotourism clearly vary, not only from one country to another, but also within the same territory. Likewise, the specific attributes of each of the markets studied, the availability of tour operators to respond to surveys depending on whether they were run in peak or low seasons and the inclusion of ecotourism products in more general products do not permit a strict comparability of the different studies presented in this series of monographs.

Readers are therefore asked to consider the results of these studies as general trends relative to the ecotourism market, rather than absolute reference data. This is the first time that such researches have been initiated. These are pioneer studies, whose methodology and results can serve as basis for future researches in this topic.

---

[1] Another WTO publication, prepared with the technical contributions of its Member States, is also devoted to the IYE. This publication, titled as "Sustainable Development of Ecotourism: A Compilation of Good Practices" (ISBN: 92-844-0478-9), contains 55 case studies from 39 countries.

Aims, definitions and methodology

After briefly summarizing the general characteristics of tourism markets, these surveys set out to analyse and evaluate, in each of the aforementioned countries, the nature tourism and ecotourism generating market, its volume, characteristics, major trends and development prospects, consumer profiles, the role of the different marketing actors, product typologies and the main communication and marketing tools used in these markets.

It was with a view to meeting these aims that WTO hired seven experts – one per country – all of whom adopted similar research methods:

- gathering the results of existing research studies with the aim of making an initial appraisal of the volume of this market;

- running consumer surveys based on a single questionnaire for all countries with a view to studying demand trends;

- running surveys among tour operators whose policies and products are commensurate, to some extent at least, with ecotourism concepts;

- studying the catalogues and brochures put out by these tour operators;

- organizing tour operator discussion forums (or focus groups) on the occasion of tourism trade fairs with a view to comparing marketing methods and results, but also with the aim of discussing the very notion of ecotourism.

It should also be noted that the same definition of ecotourism was used by all the different experts. WTO has defined this activity at two levels:

1. **Nature tourism:** a form of tourism in which the main motivation is the observation and appreciation of nature.

2. **Ecotourism:** a form of tourism with the following characteristics:

   i. All nature-based forms of tourism in which the main motivation of the tourists is the observation and appreciation of nature as well as the traditional cultures prevailing in natural areas.

   ii. It contains educational and interpretation features.

   iii. It is generally, but not exclusively, organised for small groups by specialized and small locally-owned businesses. Foreign operators of varying sizes also organize, operate and/or market ecotourism tours, generally for small groups.

   iv. It minimizes negative impacts on the natural and socio-cultural environment.

World Tourism Organization

v. It supports the protection of natural areas by:

- generating economic benefits for host communities, organizations and authorities that are responsible for conserving natural areas;

- creating jobs and income opportunities for local communities; and

- increasing awareness both among locals and tourists of the need to conserve natural and cultural assets.

The most outstanding results of the seven studies can be summed up as follows

1. The use of the term «ecotourism» in the marketing and promotional tools and used by tour operators is still relatively limited. It would appear that this term has not yet been integrated in the marketing strategies of the nature tourism sector.

2. Likewise, the tourism sector that most closely matches the concept of ecotourism represents a relatively small share of the market, an observation that is borne out by the small dimension of the tour operators that comprise this segment and the small number of tourists they cater for.

3. Conversely, these same tour operators apparently believe that the growth of ecotourism may outpace that of other tourism activities overall. Moreover, this growth appears to be consolidating irrespective of the destination considered. A priori, no world region appears to have a head-start although each region does have several landmark destinations.

4. The surveys conducted among the various audiences show that enthusiasm for nature tourism invariably goes hand in hand with a desire for meeting local communities and discovering different facets of their culture (gastronomy, handicrafts, customs, etc.).

5. According to tour operators, ecotourism enthusiasts are mostly people from relatively high social brackets and with relatively high levels of education; they are over 35 and women slightly outnumber men.

6. These studies also show that environmental awareness, while still in its infancy, is clearly growing.

7. As mentioned above, these initial findings must be confirmed on the basis of future studies. These preparatory surveys should nonetheless provide a springboard for a more in-depth examination of ecotourism markets, which will be one of the key elements of the World Ecotourism Summit to be held in Quebec, Canada, from 22 to 24 May 2002.

Acknowledgements

The World Tourism Organization would like to thank Mr. Ed Sanders of the Center for Sustainable Tourism, University of Colorado at Boulder, U.S.A., for the preparation of this report on behalf of WTO.

The World Tourism Organization and the authors would like to express their gratitude to all those tour operators who generously lent their time to participate in this research through the questionnaire survey.

Research for this report was undertaken by a team of U.S. experts commissioned by the World Tourism Organization, under the supervision of Mr. Eugenio Yunis, Chief, Sustainable Development of Tourism, WTO and Mr. Augusto Huescar, Chief, Market Intelligence and Promotion Section, WTO.
Mr. Philippe Lemaistre, Programme Officer at WTO, reviewed draft texts, tables and final editing of the report.

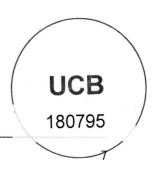

Table of Contents

List of Tables

Executive Summary

This study of the U.S. outbound ecotourism market adopts the general definition that ecotourism is a specialized form of travel to natural areas that has a number of other distinguishing characteristics. As such, "ecotourism" is just one of the many niches in the broader "nature-based" and "sustainable" tourism markets. A survey of U.S. tour operators was conducted for this study and, among other things, it confirmed that the U.S. industry generally agrees with the specific characteristics that WTO and many others have postulated for ecotourism.

One of the primary objectives of this study was to gather information on the size and growth of the U.S. outbound ecotourism market. In order to generate accurate information, a special analysis was made of the annual In-flight Survey of U.S. Travelers to Overseas and Mexico. This analysis indicated that the U.S. international ecotourism market is smaller than is generally believed and is growing at only about the same rate as tourism overall. Specifically, about four percent of U.S. international travelers participated in environmental and ecological excursions and the percentage participating in these ecotourism activities actually declined slightly between 1996 and 1999 (the end periods for which data were available). This is in sharp contrast to frequent assertions that ecotourism comprises a large and rapidly growing share of the overall tourism market.

The In-flight Survey also provides accurate information on the international destinations (excluding Canada) of U.S. ecotourists and allows a comparison with all other U.S. international air travelers. It shows that Mexico was the most popular ecotourism destination in 1999 with about a quarter of the market. Australia was a distant second (5.4%), closely followed by Jamaica and Costa Rica, with the UK, Peru, and New Zealand tied for fifth. On the other hand, when measured in terms of ecotourism orientation, U.S. ecotourists were nine times more likely to visit Kenya than the general U.S. international traveler, closely followed by Belize, New Zealand , Costa Rica and South Africa , and Chile, Peru, and Australia.

American ecotourists appeared to spend somewhat less than the general U.S. tourist, which is contrary to much of the ecotourism literature. The reported per person spending outside the United States by ecotourists was $66 per day versus $88 per day for the average U.S. traveler. These figures may overstate the difference because ecotourists are more likely to participate in package tours than the average tourist and some of the tour operators' in-country spending may not have been captured in these figures. Nonetheless, the findings suggest that U.S. ecotourists are unlikely to be significantly bigger spenders than the general tourist and may, in fact, be below the average.

The In-flight Survey indicates that the conventional wisdom that the typical ecotourist is in the 35-54 year old age bracket is somewhat misleading. Only 42% of the U.S. international ecotourists were in the 35-54 year old group, in contrast to 49% of all U.S. outbound air travelers. Or, in other words, the "Baby Boomers" are more likely to be general international tourists than they are to be ecotourists. Conversely, 34% of the U.S. ecotourists were in the 18-34 year old group (in comparison to 28% of all U.S. tourists), indicating a greater proclivity of the "Generation X'rs" to be ecotourists. Similarly, people in the older "Silent Generation" in the over 55 year old group were slightly more likely to be ecotourists (24% of the total) than the average U.S. traveler in this age group (23% of the total).

Ecotourists are usually thought to be wealthier than average. This is clearly true in comparison with the U.S. population as a whole, because international leisure travel is an expensive discretionary expenditure. However, when compared with the general U.S. international traveler, U.S. ecotourists had a slightly lower reported median household income of $79,600 versus $85,500 for the general U.S. tourist (average of 1996 and 1999 incomes). Thus, if the relevant benchmark is comparisons with that portion of the U.S. population that actually travels abroad, ecotourists do not appear to be an especially affluent segment of the effective U.S. market.

American ecotourists do stay abroad somewhat longer on their travels, with a median number of 12 nights outside of the United States versus only nine nights for the average U.S. international air traveler. In addition to longer stays, the tour operator survey indicated that their clients had a strong preference for excellent local guides, small groups, uncrowded destinations, and meaningful educational content to the trips. High quality food and accommodations and active support for conservation activities were somewhat less important. While relaxation, low cost, and sports/adventure activities rated considerably lower on client priorities. Specific activities that were most important were wildlife viewing and being in wilderness areas. These were followed by sighting rare animal species, visiting archeological sites, visiting indigenous people, bird watching, and participating in marine and other water activities. Botany and geology were considerably less important.

Perhaps the single most important finding this study is the extent to which U.S. ecotourists participated in a wide variety of other activities in addition to environmental and ecological excursions. The In-flight Survey listed two-dozen potential activities. Surprisingly, ecotourists participated more heavily in every single one of the other activities (see Table 17 in the report). As might be expected, U.S. ecotourists were more than six times as likely to go camping or hiking than the average U.S. traveler. They were five times more likely to visit national parks, three times more likely to visit ethnic heritage sites and to take ranch vacations, and twice as likely to participate in water sports and to visit cultural heritage sites.

On the other hand, U.S. ecotourists also participated more heavily in a number of activities that would not typically be associated with ecotourism, such as going to nightclubs and dancing or going to casinos and gambling. While the participation rates of ecotourists in these activities was only slightly higher than the average tourist, it suggests that most U.S. ecotourists probably fall more towards the "casual" than the "dedicated" end of the spectrum.

The U.S. ecotourists participated in an average of over ten other activities in addition to environmental and ecological excursions. On the reasonable assumption that roughly equal time was spent on each listed activity, the average U.S. ecotourist would have spent only about nine percent of his or her time on the trip engaged in ecotourism activities (or about twice that amount of time if visits to national parks and hiking and camping are also included). Perhaps more significantly, assuming equal time on each activity, the general U.S. tourist would have spent only about 0.7 percent of his or her time in ecotourism activities, suggesting the true ecotourism market may be even smaller than suggested above.

Travel agents are still the most important source of trip information for both U.S. ecotourists and general international travelers, with over half of each group using this source. On the other hand, 36 percent of the ecotourists used their personal computers to get information in 1999 (the second most widely used source of information) in contrast to only 16 percent of the general travelers. This reflects a sharp increase from 1996, when only 5.5 percent of ecotourists used their personal computers to get information. This tends to confirm the dramatic growth of the Internet and World Wide Web as a vehicle for conveying ecotourism-related information. However, only four percent of ecotourists used the Internet to actually book tickets in 1999, indicating that on-line transactions are still not widespread.

One of the outstanding issues in understanding the structure of the ecotourism market is the relative importance and role of the tour operator versus the independent traveler. The In flight Survey found that only about one-third of the U.S. ecotourists used any kind of package tour, which shows that most ecotourists make their own arrangements (although ecotourists were still almost twice as likely to use some form of package tour as the average U.S. international air traveler). This, in combination with growing use of the Internet, implies increasing opportunities for low-cost, direct marketing to the consumer.

This report confirms many of the general findings about the ecotourism market (such as preferred ecotourist activities and demographics). It does, however, suggest that U.S. international ecotourists are probably not as different from the average U.S. international traveler as is often argued. Specifically, it appears that the majority of U.S. ecotourists are probably relatively "casual" in terms of their interest in ecotourism activities in contrast to a smaller cadre of "dedicated" ecotourists. Additional research would be useful in determining just how different the attitudes, attributes, and activities of U.S. travelers falling along different parts of this spectrum really are.

Finally, this report casts considerable doubt on the widely held belief that ecotourism is a large and very rapidly growing segment of the overall tourism market. Nonetheless, true ecotourism is the best exemplar for the rest of the tourism industry for making travel and tourism more sustainable. As a result, ecotourism has an importance far greater than would be implied just by its size and rate of growth alone.

1. Introduction

1.1 Purpose of the Study

The United Nations declared 2002 to be the International Year of Ecotourism. In preparation for the event, the World Tourism Organization (WTO) commissioned a set of market studies involving seven countries (Canada, France, Germany, United Kingdom, Italy, Spain, and the United States of America). The primary goal of these studies is to help government planners and private enterprises in developing countries to evaluate the potential for ecotourism in promoting economic development and conservation. This report covers ecotourism originating from the United States.

The purpose of this study is to: clarify the definition of ecotourism; describe the size and growth of the U.S. generating ecotourism market; identify the main characteristics of that market; profile U.S. ecotourists; and summarize the main channels for marketing ecotourism products in the United States.

1.2 Territorial Coverage

The focus of the study is on ecotourists traveling from the continental United States, Hawaii, Alaska, and selected U.S. territories. Inbound and domestic ecotourism in the United States is considered when it is relevant to understanding the outbound market, but is secondary to the study of U.S. ecotourists traveling abroad. As discussed later, heavy use is made of a special analysis of the In-flight Survey of U.S. Travelers to Overseas and Mexico, conducted by the U.S. Government. This survey does not include air travel to Canada or any surface travel from the United States. As a result, the findings based on the In-flight Survey exclude all ecotourism travel to Canada and surface travel to Mexico (and the very limited surface travel to other countries via Mexico). In all other cases, statistics on U.S. outbound tourism include travel to all destinations outside of the United States.

1.3 Definition of Ecotourism in the Framework of this Study

The WTO has noted that "much has been written about ecotourism, but there is little consensus about its meaning, due to the many forms in which ecotourism activities are offered by a wide variety of operators, and practiced by an even larger array of tourists."[2] Despite the lack of a consensus definition, the report goes on to note that the general characteristics of ecotourism can be summarized as follows:

1. It includes all nature-based forms of tourism in which the main motivation of the tourists is the observation and appreciation of nature as well as the traditional cultures prevailing in natural areas.

2. It contains educational and interpretation features.

3. It is generally, but not exclusively organized for small groups by specialized and small, locally owned businesses. Foreign operators of varying sizes also organize, operate, and/or market ecotourism tours, generally for small groups.

4. It minimizes negative impacts upon the natural environment.

5. It supports the protection of natural areas by:

   • Generating economic benefits for host communities, organizations, and authorities managing natural areas with conservation purposes.

   • Providing alternative employment and income opportunities for local communities.

   • Increasing awareness towards the conservation of natural and cultural assets, both among locals and tourists.

The academic literature features numerous alternative definitions and refinements of these general characteristics of ecotourism. A few commentators also use *"ecotourism"* interchangeably, or even as synonymously, with *"nature-based tourism"* or more rarely with *"sustainable tourism"*. However, most analysts agree with the basic distinction made by the WTO and others that:

   "nature-based tourism" encompasses a broader set of activities that use natural settings as the location for an activity including those whose main purpose is recreation, personal challenge, or consumption (e.g., relaxing on beaches, sailing, climbing mountains, or hunting and fishing);

   • *"sustainable tourism"* applies to any travel, including even "mass tourism", that attempts to reduce its adverse environmental and social/cultural impacts.

---

[2] International Year of Ecotourism, 2002 (WTO and UNEP, Madrid, Spain, 2001).

This study, therefore, adopts the basic distinction that ecotourism is just one of the many niche markets within the broader nature-based and sustainable tourism categories. Beyond this fundamental categorization, academic authors have developed a number of typologies that make further distinctions as to the degree to which travel meets the tenets of ecotourism by characterizing it as "deep versus shallow", "active versus passive", "self-reliant versus popular", "hard versus soft", or "dedicated versus casual".[3] These definitions usually focus on a spectrum that ranges from travelers who are highly focused on conservation, education and/or service to those who may only be tacking an ecotourism-type activity onto an otherwise non-nature oriented trip. These types of distinctions can be helpful in evaluating market potential or designing facilities and programs to meet the needs of different segments of the ecotourism market. They also help explain the tremendous variation in estimates of the size and growth of the ecotourism market. As a result, this report occasionally uses the Lindberg definition that makes a distinction between "dedicated" versus "casual" ecotourists.

As a part of this study's effort to better understand how the term "ecotourism" is viewed within the U.S. industry, tour operators were asked to indicate what they considered to be the essential elements of ecotourism. As discussed later, the number of responses (36 responses to a questionnaire sent to 122 U.S. tour operators) precludes definitive conclusions, but the findings are probably indicative of attitudes in the U.S. industry. The tour operators were asked to rank the following characteristics of ecotourism on a scale of 1 to 5, with 1 being the most important:

• All forms of nature-based tourism in which the main motivation is the observation and appreciation of nature.

• All forms of nature-based tourism in which the main motivation is experiencing traditional cultures prevailing in natural areas.

• It minimizes negative impacts on the natural and socio-cultural environment.

• It actively supports conservation through financial or other support.

• It emphasizes generation of economic benefits to local communities

• It contains significant educational and interpretive features.

---

3   See for example, Weaver (1999), Orams (1995), and Lindberg (1991).

Table 1 (next page) shows the results of the survey of U.S. tour operators and indicates the relative importance that they attached to each of the components. In order to simplify the presentation throughout this report, all the tables based on the tour operator survey show only the most and next most important categories separately. The lower ranked responses (i.e., those ranked 3, 4, and 5) are lumped together in a single category of "lesser importance", but these individual numerical scores are still used to develop a composite average score.

The best indicator of relative importance is probably the average score, although it is instructive to look at the range of opinions as well. The respondents gave a narrow priority (average score of 1.26) to the need to avoid negative impacts on the natural and socio-cultural environments, echoing the doctor's oath of "first do no harm." According to the tour operators, it was almost as important (average score of 1.29) that ecotourism involves observing and appreciating nature. This was followed by the criterion that ecotourism actively promotes conservation. Education and interpretive aspects were ranked as the next most important. The generation of local economic benefits was deemed to be considerably less important. The cultural dimension was considered to be the least important defining characteristic of ecotourism, but still over half of the tour operators ranked it in the most important category.

Table 1   Relative Importance of Ecotourism Characteristics (Percent of respondents in each category)

	Most Important	Next Most Important	Lesser* Importance	Ave. Rank
Minimizes negative impacts	76%	21%	3%	1,26
Nature appreciation	82%	9%	9%	1.29
Promotes conservation	62%	29%	9%	1.47
Education and interpretation	56%	29%	15%	1.65
Local economic benefits	47%	26%	26%	1.79
Cultura appreciation	53%	26%	21%	1.82

Includes rankings 3, 4, and 5. Source: Tour Operator Survey, 2001. Note: not all respondents answered all questions.

The tour operators were not asked explicitly about their concurrence with the WTO characterization that ecotourism usually involves small groups, but this expectation is confirmed by the responses to the question in the survey that asked operators to rank the importance of various factors to their clients in selecting destinations. Small group size was ranked as the second most important criterion in guest preferences (after excellent local guides), see Table 16. Thus, the survey confirms that U.S. tour operators consider all the elements included in the WTO definition as being important attributes of true ecotourism.

1.4 Research Methodology and Work Undertaken

This study began with a review of the ecotourism literature. It also included a survey of tour operators, an analysis of tour operator brochures and catalogues, and focus group meetings with tour operators and travel agents. Most importantly, the study draws heavily on information specially compiled from a U.S. government survey of outbound air travelers and this data is used extensively to evaluate many aspects of the ecotourism market.

Survey of U.S. Outbound Ecotourists: In lieu of a small, one-time survey of U.S. outbound ecotourists, the WTO approved the purchase of a special analysis of the U.S. Department of Commerce's In-flight Survey of U.S. Travelers to Overseas and Mexico (hereafter referred to as the "In-flight Survey"). This survey is conducted annually by the Department's Tourism Industries office and contains a wealth of information. Use of this study allowed an "apples to apples" comparison of U.S. international ecotourists between 1996 to 1999. It also permits a level of systematic quantification of U.S. international ecotourist activities that previously has not been possible. Finally, the underlying data will continue to be collected by the U.S. Government and this will allow the time-series to be extended in the future on a consistent basis by anyone who has the interest.

As with other surveys of ecotourism, the weakness in the data stems primarily from the definition of *"ecotourism"* which is inevitably arbitrary. The annual In-flight Survey includes a set of two dozen questions about the activities that the U.S. international air traveler participated in. The survey has historically asked, among other questions, whether the travelers "visited national parks" or went "hiking or camping." These two categories certainly include a percentage of ecotourists, but they do not directly cover the more narrowly-defined target market as specified by the WTO. Instead, they are probably more indicative of the broader *"nature-tourism"* market.

In 1996, the question whether the traveler participated in "environmental or ecological excursions" was added to the In-flight Survey. This is a less-than-perfect measure of ecotourism, but it is the best proxy measure available in any U.S. government survey to date. It has the decided advantage that about 1,000 leisure travelers (and over 200 business travelers) out of a total of about 35,000 survey respondents, participated in environmental or ecological excursions. Therefore, this sample is large enough to generate statistically significant conclusions and, more importantly, it allows a comparison of ecotourists (according to this definition) to the total population of U.S. international air travelers. As shown later in the study, these comparisons suggest that American ecotourists differ from, and are similar to, the average international traveler in ways that are sometimes at odds with the conventional wisdom in the ecotourism literature.

In interpreting the results of the In-flight Survey, this report adopts the convention of categorizing all leisure (but not business) travelers who participated in environmental and ecological excursions as *"ecotourists"* and all those who visited national parks as *"nature tourists"*. This is an arbitrary distinction, but is believed to provide the best available indicator of the level and characteristics of ecotourists and nature tourists. Clearly those who participated in environmental and ecological excursions were engaged in a form of ecotourism activity but, as shown later, they also participated in a huge number of other activities (see Table 17). Unfortunately, the In-flight Survey does not ask about the primary motive of the trip, but only for a listing of all the activities that were engaged in. As a result, this category inevitably includes many travelers for whom the ecotourism activities were at most only a minor part of their travel experience. In other words, it includes a large number of casual ecotourists, some of whom were probably so peripherally involved in ecotourism activities as to hardly warrant inclusion in the category.

Conversely, an unknown percentage of visitors to national parks or people who went camping or hiking in natural areas will not have joined in formal environmental or ecological excursions. Many of these people, however, presumably participated in at least some ecotourism-type activities, but will not have been counted as ecotourists unless they responded positively to the question in the survey.

There is no way of knowing whether the number of people participating in environmental or ecological excursions understates or overstates the number of true ecotourists. However, for the purposes of this analysis, it seems reasonable to assume that the errors on both sides more or less cancel out and that this definition of ecotourists is as good as any that can realistically be devised for large surveys. In any event, the limitations from using this definition of ecotourists are believed to be far outweighed by the benefits of being able to draw on a large, statistically significant data base of U.S. outbound international air travelers that also allows systematic comparisons over time.

In order to compare ecotourists with the broader category of nature tourists, most of the tables in this report that present findings based on the In-flight Survey also provide similar figures for nature tourists (i.e., those who visited national parks while abroad). Because of the likely correlation between ecotourists and nature tourists, comparisons between the two sets of information provide a way to independently verify some of the results. (However, it is also important to note that the two data series involve double counting of those who participated in environmental/ecological excursions and those who visited national parks, so the two totals should not be added together).

Annex A presents the full findings of the special analysis. It includes subtotals for (a) ecotourists, (b) nature tourists, and a combination of (c) people who participated in environmental/ecological excursions and visited national parks and (d) people who took the excursions, visited national parks, and went camping/hiking as well as (e) all travelers. The (c) and (d) categories reflect increasingly narrow definitions of ecotourism and, therefore, are representative of more "dedicated" ecotourists. (Out of a total of 1032 ecotourists in 1999, 519 also visited national parks. Only 198 of the 1032 ecotourists participated in camping and hiking as well as visiting national parks, indicating that these multi-faceted ecotourists were relatively small in number).

The Tour Operator Survey and Brochure Analysis: In order to complement the findings of the In-flight Survey, a questionnaire was sent to 122 tour operators. 60 of the operators were members of The International Ecotourism Society (TIES) and

62 were the members of National Tour Association (NTA) who listed ecotours among the two dozen categories of tours that they offered. Only 36 responses were received and two of those responses were not included in the tallies because it appeared that the respondents were basically travel agents for whom tour operations were a secondary activity.

In all likelihood, the relatively low effective response rate (30 percent) biased the results toward the larger and more successful tour operators and towards those with a greater interest in ecotourism. This is because those operators with a stronger interest and commitment to ecotourism are the most likely to have taken the time to fill out the questionnaire, although there is no way of testing the strength of this probable bias. In addition, the analysis of the tour operator brochures (105 were received from the group of 122 operators contacted), involved a fair degree of subjectivity. For example, there was an unavoidable element of subjectivity in judging whether certain statements in the brochures should qualify as indicating a commitment by the operator to adhering to a given ecotourism principal. Similarly arbitrary decisions were required in the content analysis of photographs in the brochures whether to classify a photograph with multiple dimensions (e.g., pictures of local people or wildlife posed against spectacular natural backdrops) into one category or another. As a result, the quantitative findings from the analysis of tour operator brochures should be interpreted as being illustrative rather than definitive.

2. Overview of the U.S. Tourism Market

2.1 Historical Growth in the Outbound Market

With increasing affluence and leisure time, Americans have been traveling more abroad and venturing further afield. Over the past decade, total U.S. international travel increased by about 68 percent. The destinations have also been shifting from neighboring Canada and Mexico, where U.S. travel and tourism increased by only about 19 percent from 1990 to 2000. In contrast, American travel to more "exotic" destinations in South America, Africa, and the Middle East more than doubled in the same period and travel to Asia and Oceania almost doubled. At least part of this long-distance travel was to visit ecotourism destinations, which is the primary subject of this study.

Table 2 U.S. Resident Travel Abroad (Departures in millions)

	1990	1995	2000
Canada	12.2	13.0	15.1
Mexico	16.0	19.1	26.8
- Europe (non-add)	8.0	8.6	13.4
Caribbean	3.2	3.6	3.9
- Central America	0.6	0.8	0.9
- South America	0.9	1.6	2.1
- Africa	0.2	0.4	0.5
- Middle East	0.5	1.0	1.4
- Asia	2.5	3.6	4.9
- Oceania	0.6	0.6	1.0
Total	44.6	50.9	60.7

Source: U.S. Department of Commerce

Table 3 in the next section presents a more detailed listing of the destinations of all U.S. international travelers to overseas and Mexico. It also provides a comparison with U.S. ecotourists to these same regions and countries in order to show which destinations have been relatively more popular with American ecotourists.

2.2 Recent Trends in the U.S. Travel Market

A few of the more noteworthy domestic and international trends in U.S. tourism recently cited by the Travel Industry Association of America (TIA) [4] include:

- **Baby Boomers** (i.e., the generation born after World War II) generated the highest travel volume in the United States (registering more than 259 million trips, more than any other age group). Boomers (35-54 year-olds) are more likely to stay in a hotel or motel (60%) and to fly (26%). Boomers spend more on their trips than any other age groups, averaging $460 per trip, excluding transportation to their destination.

- **Mature Americans**, aged 55 and older, average the longest stays away from home. Half (52%) stay in hotels or motels and four in ten (43%) stay at the homes of friends or relatives. Their growing numbers coupled with their financial power and availability of time make them a very attractive market for the travel industry.

- **Honeymooners** outspent the average traveler by more than three times. On average, the spent $1,402 while the average trip expenditure in 1994 for all travelers was considerably less at $421.

- **Children** make frequent travel companions. Nearly one-half (46%) of U.S. adults said that they included a child or children on a trip in the past five years and sixteen percent included grandchildren.

- **Weekend Trips** by Americans jumped by 70 percent between 1986 and 1996 and now account for more than half of all U.S. travel. In comparison, non-weekend travel increased by only 15 percent during the same period. Americans took 604 million weekend person trips in 1996 and nearly 80 percent of the travel was for pleasure. Weekend trips are popular year round, but summer is the most popular time for weekend travel, accounting for 28 percent of all weekend trips.

- **Shopping** continues to be the most popular trip activity by U.S. adult travelers, and accounts for one-third of all person trips. But travelers do more than just shop while on vacation. One in five person-trips including shopping also includes visits to historical places or museums. Other top activities by U.S. shoppers are outdoor recreation, visits to National or State Parks, and visiting theme parks.

- **Adventure Travelers** are everywhere. One-half of U.S. adults, or 98 million people, have taken an adventure trip in the past five years. This includes 31 million adults who engaged in hard adventure activities like whitewater rafting, scuba diving, and mountain biking. Adventure travelers are more likely to be young, single, and employed, compared to all U.S. adults.

---

[4]   See www.tia.org/Travel/TravelTrends.asp

World Tourism Organization

- **National Parks** are one of America's biggest attractions. Nearly 30 million U.S. adults took a trip of 100 miles or more, one-way, to visit a national park during the past year. A large share of these travelers (70%) participated in outdoor activities while visiting the national parks. Among these outdoor activities, hiking (53%) was the most popular, followed by camping (33%) and fishing (19%).

- **Camping** is the number one outdoor activity in America. One-third of U.S. adults say they have gone on a camping vacation in the past five years. Camping vacationers tend to be married with children at home. The average age of travelers who go camping is 37 and their median household income is $43,000.

- **Biking** vacations attracted more than 27 million travelers in the past five years and they rank as the third most popular outdoor vacation activity in America. People who take biking trips tend to be young and affluent. About half are between the ages of 18 and 34 and one-fourth are from households with incomes of $75,000 or more.

- **Cultural and Historic Tours** is one of the more popular sectors of the travel industry. A recent TIA survey found that 54 million adults said that they visited a museum or historic site in the past year and 33 million adults attended a cultural event such as a theater, arts, or music festival. Cultural and historic travelers spend more, stay in hotels more often, and visit more destinations.

- **Educational Travel** is important to U.S. travelers. About one-fifth – 30 million adults – have taken an educational trip to learn or improve a skill, sport, or hobby in the past three years. Eighteen percent of travelers in the past year said that taking such a trip was the main purpose of their travel and they tend (51%) to have a household income of over $75,000.

- **Garden Tours** are popular with many travelers. Nearly 40 million Americans went on a garden tour, visited a botanical garden, attended a gardening show, or participated in some other garden-related activity in the past five years. About one-third of the garden travelers have a household income of above $75,000.

- **Fitness** while Traveling: More than one-fourth of U.S. travelers – 25 million adults – used a fitness center or gym while traveling in the past three years.

- **The Internet** tends to be popular with travelers who are computer savvy. Two-thirds of the 90 million travelers who are online – over 59 million—used the Internet to make travel plans in 2000. Use of the Internet to actually book travel continues to increase, with 27 percent of all travelers now online having made travel reservations on the Internet during the past year. That is up nearly 60 percent over 1999.

2.3 Expected U.S. Tourism Growth

This report was finalized shortly after the terrorist attack on the World Trade Center towers and the Pentagon. The immediate impact was a substantial reduction in U.S. international and domestic travel, especially air travel. It is too early to predict whether the chilling effect of these attacks will last for an extended period, whether there will be new attacks in the United States or abroad, and how quickly confidence in the safety of air travel and various destinations can be restored. In addition, based on the preliminary indicators, the U.S. economy has slipped into a recession of unknown depth and duration. As a result, forecasts of domestic or outbound tourism growth from the United States are subject to far more uncertainty than usual. An analysis to attempt to narrow the range of that uncertainty is beyond the scope of this report.

3. The United States Ecotourism Market

3.1 Demand Estimates

It is widely accepted, and often repeated as fact, that ecotourism is one of, if not the, largest and fastest growing segments of the tourism industry. Many books and articles refer to "the recent boom in ecotourism", state that ecotourism has been growing at "explosive rates", or make similar references to very fast growth.[5] These assessments are not new. For instance, in the early 1990s, Fillion and colleagues estimated that nature tourism (often inappropriately interpreted as synonymous with the narrower concept of ecotourism) accounted for 40-60 percent of the tourism market and that wildlife viewing accounted for 20-40 percent of the market.[6] About the same time, the World Resources Institute estimated that the ecotourism market was growing at 15 to 30 percent annually. These statistics have been cited repeatedly by many other authors and have probably become the most widely quoted estimates of market size and growth in the industry.[7] Other sources have suggested somewhat slower growth rates, such as 10-25 percent, but virtually all echo the view that ecotourism is growing much more rapidly than the overall tourism market.[8] One commentator has pointed out that the assertion that ecotourism is the fastest growing form of tourism is "surprising and equally suspect" given the "lack of consensus over its definitions" and the "serious deficiency in quantitative evidence and analysis" but this view is in the decided minority.[9]

---

[5]   See, for example, McCool.

[6]   See Fillion et al.

[7]   See, for example, The International Ecotourism Society Website at www.ecotourism.org.

[8]   See, for example, citations in Lindberg (1997)

[9]   Weaver (1999)

Casual observation and "back of the envelope" projections certainly suggest that caution should be exercised in accepting assertions that ecotourism constitutes a major portion of the market and that it is growing much more rapidly than the industry as a whole. For example, if the broader nature tourism market had actually comprised 40 percent of the total in 1990 and had grown at 30 percent annually over the last decade, its share of the market would have increased to around 85 percent of the total market in 2000. Common sense suggests that nature tourism (much less true ecotourism) could not comprise such a large percentage of the market, since business travel alone would take up more than the remaining market. This would have left no room at all for so-called "mass tourism". Thus, at a minimum, the conventional wisdom that nature tourism and/or ecotourism comprise a sizable share of the international tourism market and have been growing much more rapidly than the overall tourism market, warrants critical review.

The challenge in estimating the growth in demand for worldwide ecotourism is that no data exist to measure ecotourism based on any operationally rigorous definitions. As a result, we have to fall back on proxy measures for the growth of ecotourism.

The U.S. Outbound Market: The best available indicator for U.S. outbound ecotourism is from the annual survey of international air passengers conducted by the U.S. Department of Commerce's International Trade Administration (the In-flight Survey Data: U.S. Travelers to Overseas and Mexico). As noted earlier, this survey covers only air passengers, and excludes air travel to Canada (reportedly because Canada collects good incoming air passenger data) and excludes all surface travel abroad, which effectively means that it overlooks all eco-travel to Canada and an unknown portion of eco-travel to Mexico. Nonetheless, the In-flight Survey provides a systematic and statistically valid survey of about 35,000 passengers annually and provides an accurate reflection of U.S. tourism outside of North America, since virtually all travel to these destinations is by air.

One of the questions that the survey asks is what leisure activities the traveler participated in. Twenty-four possible activities are listed ranging from dining in restaurants to snow skiing (see Table 17 for a listing of the activities). In 1996, the survey added the question whether the traveler participated in "Environmental/Ecological Excursions" in order to try to identify those passengers who were engaged in ecotourism activities. This definition is somewhat restrictive in that some passengers may have engaged in ecotourism-type activities without formally joining in environmental or ecological "excursions", but it is the best proxy among the listed questions for measuring ecotourism. As a result, as noted earlier, whenever using data from the In-flight Survey, this study refers to all leisure travelers who participated in these excursions as "ecotourists."

In 1996 (the first year that the category was added) 4.8 percent of U.S. outbound air passengers reported that they participated in environmental or ecological excursions. By 1999, that percentage had actually dropped to 4.2 percent of the total, although preliminary 2000 data indicates that the percentage had risen back to the five percent range (i.e., somewhere between 4.5 and 5.5 percent). There will inevitably be year-to-year fluctuation because the number of passengers engaging in Environmental/Ecological Excursions is relatively small (about one thousand). Nonetheless, by this definition at least, outbound ecotourism over the past four or five years appears to have been growing at only about the same rate as overall U.S. outbound air tourism. As the only hard data on U.S. outbound ecotourism, the evidence does not support those who have asserted that ecotourism (at least from the United States) is one of the fastest growing segments of the tourism market.

For comparative purposes, it is also instructive to note that the In-flight Survey indicated that the percent of U.S. international travelers who visited foreign national parks fell from 8.9 percent in 1996 to 8.4 percent in 1999. The share of U.S. international travelers who participated in camping/hiking also fell slightly from 4.8 percent to 4.7 percent over the same period. While the visitors to national parks and the camper/hikers are classified as "nature tourists" for the purposes of this study, there is likely a high correlation between people participating in these activities and "ecotourists". This provides a partial, but independent validation of the hypothesis that outbound U.S. ecotourism was probably only growing at about the same rate as overall outbound U.S. tourism, at least since 1996.

The survey of U.S. tour operators provides mixed evidence regarding the rate at which U.S. outbound ecotourism has been growing. Twenty-two of the 34 respondents (65 percent of the total) indicated that ecotourism had been a relatively constant share of their business over the past five years. Ten (29 percent) indicated that the ecotourism share of their business had been increasing, while two (6 percent) reported that it was declining. The fact that over one quarter of the operators reported that ecotourism was an increasing rather than decreasing share of their business could be interpreted as an indicator of higher relative growth in ecotourism. On the other hand, as noted earlier, the tour operator survey is likely to be biased to an unknown degree toward the more committed, and probably faster growing, companies and probably does not accurately reflect industry-wide trends.

On balance, therefore, American tourists visiting overseas are quite unlikely to have been the source the often-cited "recent boom" or "explosive growth" in ecotourism. Similarly, the limited available evidence does not support the contention that inbound ecotourism or domestic ecotourism in the United States accounts for a sizable portion of the overall tourism market or that it has been booming.

Inbound and Domestic Ecotourism: The In-flight Survey of inbound passengers, reveals essentially similar results as the outbound survey. In both 1999 and 2000, only three percent of the foreign visitors flying into the United States participated in environmental or ecological excursions. This compares to the fully 20 percent who visited U.S. National Parks and to the four percent who visited American Indian Communities and the four percent who went camping/hiking. Thus, it seems reasonable to conclude that ecotourism is a relatively minor element in the overall mix of U.S. tourism attractions. However, it is important to note that the U.S. national park system is a much bigger draw for foreigners visiting the United States than are foreign national parks for Americans going abroad. Twenty percent of foreign air travelers visited U.S. parks, but only eight percent of outbound Americans air travelers visited national parks overseas. Thus, to the extent that visitors to national parks can be characterized as nature tourists rather than ecotourists, the broader category of nature tourism to the United States may be significantly more important than the more narrowly defined ecotourism.

Over the past ten years, recreational visits to U.S. National Parks, which are generally considered to be the crown-jewels of American nature destinations, have been relatively flat. Total visits (which include both in-bound and domestic tourists) in 1990 were 268 million and rose only to 286 million in 2000. This is an increase of just over half of one percent per year, which is well below population growth, implying a decline in per capita recreational visits to the National Parks over the past decade. Thus, based solely on visits to the U.S. national parks, the domestic and in-bound nature tourism market would seem to have been growing less rapidly than the overall tourism market. To the extent that ecotourism trends parallel the broader nature tourism category, it would also appear that domestic ecotourism is likely to have been relatively flat.

Whatever the mix of ecotourists and nature tourists, their importance should not be double counted to the extent that the two groups overlap. Moreover, these tourists engage in a very wide variety of other activities as well (see Table 17 for detail). As a result, it may be more appropriate to count only the portion of their time that they spent visiting the parks or engaged in environmental or ecological excursions when estimating the growth and size of the ecotourism and nature tourism markets.

In summary, while the United States is often characterized as the largest source market for ecotourism, it does not appear to have been the engine behind the frequently-reported high growth in global ecotourism over the last 5-10 years. If ecotourism has in fact actually been "booming" in recent years, the source of that growth will have had to originate in other countries. It is beyond the scope of this study to identify the sources of demand for worldwide ecotourism.

3.2 Typology of Ecotourism Products

As noted above, the academic literature is filled with numerous typologies for characterizing ecotourism products and the potential ways of segmenting the ecotourism market seem almost endless. This report concentrates on several of the more important dimensions of ecotourism.

The first categorization is by destination. The next section of the report identifies the main ecotourism destinations by geographic region and key countries. It also compares the destinations of U.S. outbound ecotourists with all other U.S. international air travelers in order to get a rough comparison of how they differ. The report does not attempt to further quantify U.S. outbound ecotourism submarkets by breaking them down into the types of destinations (e.g., marine, mountain, jungle, desert) because no good data sources were found.

A second way of categorizing ecotourism is by the level of service being offered. This is a more subjective measure and there is lots of overlap in categories, but section 3.4 attempts to shed some light on this issue. The tour operators were asked whether their target markets were high-end (i.e., luxury), mid-level, or budget-oriented. A slight majority of the operators targeted the mid-level market, with most of the rest serving the high-end market. However, only about one-third of ecotourists appear to travel with operators (see Table 28) so an important question remains regarding the level of service being sought by independent travelers.

A third typology, therefore, considers the nature of the ecotourist's travel arrangements. Traditionally, the travel industry has divided the market between free and independent travelers (FITs) and group travelers. Again, the categories overlap in many ways and the data are not good. Section 4.1 addresses the issue from both the tour operator perspective and In-flight Surveys, with differing results. It appears most likely that FITs comprise about two-thirds of the U.S. outbound ecotourism market, so tour operator surveys miss a substantial portion of the market.

A fourth set of typologies focuses on ecotourism demographics and other characteristics of the traveler. These are covered at length in Section 4.1. One aspect of most of these typologies that traditionally gets little attention is the extent to which ecotourism is the primary purpose of a trip versus just an ancillary element. This report stresses the importance of distinguishing between "dedicated" versus "casual" ecotourists, since confusion over who should be considered a true ecotourist probably accounts for much of the huge variation in estimates of the size and growth of the ecotourism market. The In-flight Survey provides some especially interesting information in this regard in terms of the large number of activities engaged in by the typical ecotourist. For example, Table 17 indicates that they averaged over ten other activities per trip in addition to participating in environmental or ecological excursions.

3.3 Main Foreign and Domestic Ecotourism Destinations

The In-flight Survey provides the best quantitative estimates of the relative importance of ecotourism destinations. As previously noted, it excludes Canada and an unknown portion of ecotourists to Mexico, where Americans are likely to drive to northern desert and coastal destinations, but fly to the larger ecotourism destinations in the Yucatan and the south. With these exceptions, the survey indicates that U.S. eco-travelers are participating in environmental and ecological excursions all over the world. The ecotourists are largely concentrating in the areas and countries where it would be expected. Table 3 (next page) shows the destinations of ecotourists in comparison to all leisure tourists in 1999. The sample of ecotourists responding to this question was relatively small (996) so the number going to any particular country is often less than a dozen. As a result, the specific percentages of ecotourists for each country should be considered illustrative rather than definitive, since they can change significantly from year to year just because of sampling variation.

There are essentially two ways to interpret the table. The first way is by ranking the countries in terms of the absolute number of U.S. tourists participating in environmental and ecological excursions. By this measure, Mexico swamps the other countries and accounts for over one-quarter of the ecotourists. Australia is a distant second (5.4%), closely followed by Jamaica (5.1%), and Costa Rica (4.0%), with the UK, Peru, and New Zealand tied for fifth (3.9%). Several of these leading countries, such as Mexico, Jamaica and the UK probably feature relatively "soft" ecotourism excursions that appeal primarily to the "casual" ecotourist, whereas others, such as Costa Rica and Peru are well-known ecotourism destinations. If 1996 data is used (see Annex A for details), the rankings change somewhat. Mexico continues to be the dominant ecotourism destination, with almost a quarter of the total. Peru moves ahead of Australia into second place (with 5.4% versus 5.1%), suggesting that shifts of a percentage point or two will not be unusual from year-to-year in part because of the small sample size for each individual country.

Table 3   Main Destination of Ecotourists and All Leisure Travelers (Percent or respondents in each category)

Destination	% Ecotourists	% All Tourists
Western Europe	16.7	36.7
- Germany	2.0	4.6
- France	1.9	4.4
- United Kingdon	3.9	10.4
- Eastern Europe	0.5	1.7
Caribbean	12.4	14.5
- Bahamas	2.3	4.3
- Jamaica	5.1	5.1
South America	12.4	6.5
- Argentina	1.2	0.8
- Brazil	1.5	1.6
- Chile	1.5	0,4
- Ecuador	1.5	0,7
- Peru	3.9	1.1
Central America	30.9	21.7
- Belize	0.8	0.1
- Costa Rica	4.0	1.0
- Other (includes Mexico)	25.8	19.4
Africa	5.2	1.4
- Kenya	1.8	0.2
- South Africa	1.7	0.4
Middle East	2.7	3.0
Asia	9.6	3.0
- India	2.3	1.3
Oceania	10.0	2.6
- Australia	5.4	1.6
- New Zealand	3.9	0.8

Source: In-flight Survey

The second way of interpreting the table is to identify those countries which feature ecotourism as a major component of their overall tourism offering. By this measure the rankings are quite different. Kenya appears to be the most oriented toward U.S. ecotourism (U.S. ecotourists were roughly 9 times more likely to visit the country in 1999 than the average U.S tourist) closely followed by Belize (x 8). New Zealand was the next most U.S. ecotourism-intensive destination (x 5), followed by Costa Rica and South Africa (x 4) and by Chile, Peru, and Australia (x 3). Ecuador was the only other country where U.S. ecotourists appeared to more than twice as likely to visit as the general tourist. The specific rankings change somewhat if the 1996 data is used, but the same countries emerge as the ecotourism leaders by this relative measure. This provides some validation of it usefulness as a rough indicator of the relative attractiveness of various destinations to U.S. travelers participating in environmental and ecological excursions.

The relative attractiveness of various ecotourism attractions can also be assessed though a content analysis of the sample brochures received from the tour operators. While this assessment is inherently more subjective, it does present a sense of where the tour operators see the best business opportunities for their services. This analysis presents a somewhat different picture by region. As compared to the In-flight Survey, the brochures (weighted by the number of operators offering tours to each area, excluding the United States and Canada) tended to give greater emphasis to trips to South America, Africa, Asia, and Oceania than would be implied by the In-flight Survey. Conversely, the brochures tended to give relatively less emphasis to Europe, and to the Caribbean, Central America, and Mexico. This is not surprising, since travelers from the United States will generally be more familiar with these destinations, which are also more accessible, and therefore less likely to rely on tour operators to arrange their trips.

Table 4   Regional preferences (Percent in each category)

	Tour Operator Brochures	In-Flight Survey
Caribbean, Mexico and Cent. America	23%	43%
Europe	9%	17%
South America	21%	12%
Africa	18%	8%
Asia	15%	9%
Oceania (includes Antarctica)	14%	10%

Source: Tour Operator Brochures & In-flight Survey

3.4 Pricing

One complication in evaluating the pricing of ecotourism products is the wide variety of complementary services that must be included in evaluating the overall cost of an international ecotourism trip. Most trips include airfare to get to the site, local transportation, lodging, tours, and the costs of all the other activities that the ecotourist participates in. It appears that only about one-third of the ecotourists surveyed used packaged tours (see Table 29 below). In the remaining cases, the components will have been purchased separately. The In-flight Survey did not ask for information on pricing of these component elements, but only on the overall cost of the trip. It did show the various combinations of elements that travelers bundled together in their package purchases, but it was not possible to separate the various components in terms of each of their prices.

An interesting finding of the In-flight Survey is that, on the surface, ecotourists appear to spend somewhat less than the average tourist. As shown in Table 5, the reported per person daily spending outside the United States in 1999 was $66 for the ecotourist versus $84 for the average traveler. (In 1996, the reported difference was even greater, with reported spending of only $53 for the ecotourist in comparison with $81 for the average traveler). It may, therefore, be that ecotourism is failing in one of its primary goals of generating higher economic benefits for the local population, as indicated by per day or per trip spending outside the United States. Before jumping to that conclusion, however, it should also be noted that the reported spending by the one-third of ecotourists who traveled on group tours may not have included the tour company's expenditures outside the United States in their estimates. This could significantly bias the results, since more ecotourists than average tourists took package tours (see Table 29). In this regard, one of the tour operators in the focus group meeting emphasized his company's commitment to channeling as much spending as possible into the local economy. He estimated that over 60 percent of total tour expenditures were in the host country and that much of that went to local communities. To the extent that this performance is typical, ecotourists may in fact spend more per day in local communities – directly and indirectly – than the average American international traveler.

Table 5   Total Trip Expenditures (per visitor)

	% of Ecotourists	% of Nature Tourists	% of all Travelers
Mean Total Trip Expend.	$2,435	$2,737	$2,534
Mean Package Price	$2,687	$3,601	$1,871
Mean Expend. outside U.S.	-	-	-
per visitor trip	$1,097	$1,263	$1,167
per visitor day	$66	$60	$84

Source: In-flight Survey

As an interesting side-note, the In-flight Survey indicated a noticeable shift in the means of payment between 1996 and 1999. Among both ecotourists and all international travelers, credit and debit cards were becoming more popular, while the use of travelers checked dropped sharply. This suggests that any ecotourism companies wishing to attract U.S. tourists should make arrangements to accept credit and debit cards as a means of payment.

Table 6   Means of Payment (1996 and 1999)

	1996 Ecotourists	1999 Ecotourists	1996 all Travelers	1999 all Travelers
Credit Cards	41%	46%	50%	53%
Travelers Checks	18%	13%	12%	8%
Debit Cards	2%	4%	2%	4%
Cash	39%	36%	36%	35%

Source: In-flight Survey

3.5 Future Trends

As noted earlier, this report was finalized shortly after the terrorist attack on the World Trade Center and the Pentagon. The impact of the attack makes uncertain the immediate and mid-term prospects for U.S. outbound ecotourism. For the next few months, the primary question will be just how deep the reductions in tourism will be – and the outlook two months after the attack is not promising. Over the medium term, how long it will take for the U.S. international tourism market to bounce back will depend on whether and where additional terrorist attacks occur and how successful governments around the world will be in implementing meaningful protective measures and in rebuilding public confidence.

Over the longer-term (i.e., the next few decades), it seems likely that ecotourism will be a robust, although not dramatically increasing, segment of the overall tourism market. The most important reason for this is demographics. The baby boom is entering the age brackets where people have more discretionary income and, as people move into retirement, have the leisure time to devote to travel and a variety of self-improvement projects. As the ecotourism market ages, the pattern of activities will shift from the more active pursuits that appeal to the younger adventure traveler to more sedentary and educational activities, such as bird-watching or service vacations, that appeal to the older segments of the ecotourism market.

Absent major international conflict, the forces of globalization will open more destinations to increasing numbers of people. This will pose a challenge for the "world-class" destinations such as the Galapagos Islands, some of Africa's game parks, or Yellowstone National Park, which will have to cope with increasing crowds and visitor management problems. On the other hand, U.S. ecotourists give a high priority to wilderness experiences and to going to new and unusual places. This suggests that many currently under-appreciated areas may be able to better capitalize on their ecotourism potential and realize the economic and conservation benefits that are currently accruing to the more popular destinations without suffering from the same degree of overcrowding.

4. U.S. Ecotourist Characteristics

4.1 Ecotourist Characteristics

Ecotourists are generally believed to be somewhat older, better educated, and higher income that the average. This is clearly the case in comparison with the overall U.S. populatoin, but not necessarily so in comparison with the international traveling public, which is more similar to the profile of outbound ecotourists. This report suggests that it is more relevant to compare U.S. international ecotourists with other international travelers from the United States than with the American population as a whole, because many Americans will probably never travel abroad and are not good prospects for ecotourism or any other form of international tourism.

U.S. ecotourists are somewhat more balanced in terms of the sex of travelers than the average U.S. international traveler. Sixty percent of all U.S. outbound air travelers in the In-flight Survey were male, whereas only 54 percent of the ecotourists were male. However, these statistics still suggest a heavier preponderance of males in ecotourism than most other studies, which have suggested a roughly even split or even a slight majority of females.[10] Table 7 also presents an interesting split by age. The proportion of ecotourists to all travelers is higher for both males and females in the younger groups (ages 18-34). However the pattern Is strikingly different for males 45 and older, who are generally considered to be prime ecotourism candidates market. They are significantly less likely to participate in ecotourism excursions than the average male traveler of the same age. Conversely, females 45 and older age groups appear significantly more likely to participate in ecotourism excursions than the general female traveler of the same age.

---

[10] The International Ecotourism Society Statistical Fact Sheet, available at www.ecotourism.org

Table 7   Sex and Age of U.S. Traveler (1999)

	% Male Ecotourists	% all Male Travelers	% Female Ecotourists	% all Female Travelers
% Total	54.2	59.9	45.8	40.1
18-24 years	4.2	3.2	4.0	3.8
25-29 years	5.5	5.1	7.7	4.7
30-34 years	6.9	6.5	5.5	5.0
35-39 years	5.9	7.9	3.6	4.9
40-44 years	6.1	7.9	2.6	5.2
45-49 years	5.9	7.3	4.9	4.1
50-54 years	7.5	7.5	5.8	4.2
55-64 years	7.9	9.3	8.5	5.3
65 + years	4.3	5.3	3.4	2.9
Mean Age (years)	43.7	44.9	42.9	42.3

Source: In-flight Survey

Another way of arraying the data in Table 7 is by broader age cohort. In the United States, much attention has been paid to the "baby boom" generation born after World War II (ages 35-54). Somewhat less attention has been paid to the subsequent generation — often called "Generation X" (ages 18-34) — or to the preceding generation (the "Silent Generation" (ages 55-74). Many sources, such as The International Ecotourism Society, state that the typical ecotourist is in the 35-54 age bracket, i.e., that they are baby boomers.11   However, if we array U.S. outbound ecotourists by generation, we find that well under half (42%) of the ecotourists were baby boomers. Perhaps even more interesting, in comparison to the typical U.S. international traveler, it appears that the baby boomers are proportionately less likely to participate in environmental or ecological excursions than their younger or older counterparts. For instance, Table 8 indicates that only 42 percent of the baby boomers participated in ecotourism activities even though they constituted 49 percent of all U.S. international travelers. In contrast, 34 percent of Generation X'ers participated in ecotourism activities, but constituted only 28 percent of all U.S. international travelers. Similarly, the older generation was slightly more likely to participate in ecotourism activities relative to their overall weight in outbound travel (24 versus 23 percent).

Table 8   Age Distribution by Generation (1999)

	% Male. Ecotour.	% All Males	% Female Ecotour.	% All Females	% Ecotour.	% All Travelers
18-34 years	16.6	14.7	17.2	13.5	33.8	28.2
35-54 years	25.4	30.6	16.8	18.4	42.2	49.0
over 55	12.2	14.6	11.8	8.2	24.0	22.8
Total	54.2	59.9	45.8	40.1	100.0	100.0

Source: In-flight Survey

In summary, the In-flight Survey presents a very different picture of the age profile of U.S. ecotourists than the conventional wisdom. For example, the excellent and widely quoted Canadian study of North American ecotourists conducted in 1994 found that 56 percent of the Canadian and American ecotourists were in the 35-54 age bracket in contrast to only 43 percent of the general consumers.12 Since the findings of the In-flight Survey are so at odds with the consensus profile of ecotourists in the research community, they should not be accepted uncritically. They do, however, suggest that when measured by a representative sample of actual U.S. outbound air travelers, the characteristics of U.S. international ecotourists are considerably different than has been widely accepted. At a minimum, further research would be useful in order to determine why the prevailing assessments seem to be so different from the findings from the In-flight Survey.

Typically the data for ecotourists and all travelers is relatively consistent between 1996 and 1999. In order to simplify the presentation, this report usually presents data for only 1999 (complete data for both years is detailed in Annex A). In the case of income, a substantial discrepancy exists between the two years. Table 8, therefore, presents the annual household income of the travelers for both years.

In 1996, the average income of the ecotourists (as well as the nature tourists) was substantially lower than the average of all U.S. international outbound travelers. In contrast, the mean income for U.S. ecotourists in 1999 was slightly above the average (although median was slightly below). The main reason for the difference is that, compared to the average traveler, ecotourists were significantly less likely to have incomes over $200,000 in 1996 whereas they were much more likely than the average to have incomes over that level in 1999. Ecotourists were also over-represented in the lower income categories (i.e., under ($60,000) in 1996, but were proportionately less likely to be in these categories in 1999. Potential explanations for this rapid shift in relative incomes between ecotourists and all travelers are not clear, especially since the sample size is large enough to reduce the likelihood of simple sampling error.

Table 9   Annual Household Income of Traveler (1996 and 1999)

	% 1996 Ecotourists	% 1996 all Travelers	% 1999 Ecotourists	% 1999 all Travelers
Under $20,000	5.1	4.9	3.0	4.1
$20,000-39,999	15.1	12.8	7.8	10.8
$40,000-59,999	20.1	16.3	14.4	15.4
$60,000-79,999	18.2	15.1	19.2	13.8
$80,000-99,999	10.6	12.2	12.7	12.3
$100-000-119,999	9.1	9.8	9.8	10.9
$120,000-139,999	4.3	6.6	6.8	6.6
$140,000-159,999	4.5	4.9	4.6	5.2
$160,000-179,999	2.9	2.5	1.1	3.2
$180,000-199,999	1.9	2.0	0.6	2.5
Over $200,000	8.4	12.9	20.0	15.3
Mean Income	$85,600	$96,000	$106,200	102,600
Median Income	$70,700	$81,500	$88,600	89,500

Source: In-flight Survey

If the 1996 data are used, U.S. ecotourists going abroad had a lower income than the average international U.S. traveler. Even if the 1999 data are used, ecotourists had a household income that was about average for all international travelers. Most analyses of ecotourism assert that ecotourists have above average incomes and are, therefore, an especially attractive market segment. However, if compared to the average international traveler, the In-flight Survey suggests that ecotourists seem to have roughly equal or even somewhat lower household incomes than the average American who flies abroad.

The In-flight Survey also suggests that the occupations of ecotourists are not that different from the average U.S. international outbound traveler. Ecotourists were significantly less likely to be in the Manager/Executive category (20 percent versus 30 percent). This is partly the result of the higher manager/executive travel in the business category, which is included in "all" column but not the ecotourism totals. Otherwise the differences by occupation do not seem to be that substantial, as shown in Table 10.

Table 10 Occupation of U.S. Travelers (1999)

	% of Ecotourists	% of Nature Tourists	% of all Travelers
Clerical/Sales	7.1	5.2	5.3
Craftsman/Factory Work	4.1	4.4	3.4
Government/Military	2.0	2.0	1.9
Homemaker	3.6	6.7	5.6
Manager/Executive	19.8	17.9	29.7
Professional/Technical	42.4	39.1	37.7
Retired	12.8	15.0	9.6
Student	7.6	8.1	5.9
Other	0.6	1.5	0.8

Source: In-flight Survey

Ecotourists are significantly more likely to travel with their spouses, family, and/or friends than the average U.S. outbound traveler. Almost half of the ecotourists travelled with their spouses, in comparison to only a little over one-quarter of all U.S. international travelers. Furthermore, the ecotourism party averaged 1.9 people in comparison with 1.5 people in the typical U.S. international party. U.S. international ecotourists were somewhat more likely to be traveling with children in contrast to the average party (9.6 percent versus 6.7 percent of the parties included children). Conversely, only one in five of the ecotourists was traveling alone versus almost two out of five of all travelers.

Table 11 Travel companions (1999)

	% of Ecotourists	% of Nature Tourists	% of all Travelers
Business Associates	0.8	0.3	6.7
Family/Relative	28.0	27.9	21.8
Friends	18.1	17.3	12.2
Spouse	48.7	42.3	29.4
Tour Group	3.3	2.7	2.3
Traveling Alone	21.5	25.8	39.4
Traveling with Children	9.6	9.8	6.7
Average Group Size (#)	1.9	1.8	1.5

Source: In-flight Survey

Ecotourists stayed slightly longer on their trips than typical U.S. travelers, averaging almost 17 days per trip outside the United States versus 14 for all travelers (with a median number of nights of 12 versus 9 for all travelers). Nature tourists seemed to stay even longer. As shown in the full report (Annex A), the mean number of nights for the average traveler dropped between 1996 and 1999 (from 15.4 to 13.9) but rose slightly for ecotourists (16.2 to 16.9) and for nature tourists (from 19.3 to 21.1). As a result, the evidence suggests that the oft-cited move toward shorter vacations may not apply to U.S. international ecotourists and nature tourists.

Table 12 Nights Outside of the United States (1999)

	% of Ecotourists	% of Nature Tourists	% of all Travelers
1-3 Night	6.8	3.2	10.4
4-7 Nights	25.4	14.2	32.6
8-10 Nights	14.3	13.5	16.2
11-14 Nights	16.9	17.9	15.3
15-21 Nights	20.8	24.8	13.7
22-28 Nights	4.7	7.0	3.2
29-35 Nights	3.7	11.3	4.2
36 or more Nights	7.3	8.2	4.5
Mean # of Nights	16.7	21.1	13.9
Median # of Nights	12.0	15.0	9.0

Source: In-flight Survey

U.S. ecotourists and nature tourists appear to be less frequent international travelers than the average U.S. international traveler. For example, as shown in Table 13, ecotourists averaged two international trips in the past year and seven in the past five years in comparison with three trips in the last year and almost twelve trips in the past five years for the average international traveler. This may be explained at least partially by the fact that the "all travelers" category includes business travelers who tend to travel more often. Nonetheless, the data suggest that ecotourists travel less-frequently (although stay somewhat longer) than the average American international traveler.

Table 13 International Travel Experience (1999)

	Ecotourists	Nature Tourists	All Travelers
First International Trip -- Yes	6.1%	7.5%	6.2%
First International Trip -- No	93.9%	92.5%	93.8%
# of Trips in Last 12 Months	2.1	2.0	3.2
# of Trips in Last 5 Years	7.3	7.2	11.9

Source: In-flight Survey

The In-flight Survey provides information on the state (and in some cases, the city) of origin of international passengers. Table 14 summarizes the results by region and shows the states of California and New York as well, since they are by far the two largest originating states. (Information for each state of origin is included in Annex A). The results show some interesting trends. For example, leisure travelers from the Middle Atlantic (including New York) are significantly less likely to participate in the ecotourism and nature tourism activities than their counterparts from the Mountain West and Pacific Coast states. This is probably to be expected in view of the more outdoor-oriented lifestyles of the West. Therefore, when faced with budget constraints, ecotourism marketing should generally emphasize those regions and states that have the highest participation rates in ecotourism-type activities.

Table 14 Region/State of Residence of Ecotourists (1999)

	% of Ecotourists	% of Nature Tourists	% of all Travelers
New England	9.6	7.4	8.9
Middle Atlantic	20.5	17.1	22.5
New York (non-add)	(10.4)	(9.6)	(13.8)
East North Central	9.6	10.9	10.0
West North Central	3.1	3.5	2.9
South Atlantic	13.9	11.5	15.8
East South Central	1.1	2.2	1.8
West South Central	5.9	6.4	7.9
Mountain	7.6	9.5	5.9
Pacific	27.9	29.5	23.0
California (non-add)	(23.1)	(23.8)	(19.7)

Source: In-flight Survey

4.2 Ecotourist Motivations

The In-flight survey provides some general insights into the motivations of ecotourists (as defined in this study to include only those travelers who participated in environmental and ecological excursions) in terms of the purposes of the trip. In comparison with nature tourists and especially in comparison with all travelers, ecotourists appear to have been somewhat more focused on leisure, recreation, and holidays. Nonetheless, as shown in Table 15, ecotourists still appeared to be motivated by a number of other considerations, most importantly visiting friends and relatives, but also other activities such as conducting business and study/teaching activities. These other activities, suggest that many ecotourists are engaged in multi-purpose vacations, which adds some additional support for the hypothesis that many, if not most, ecotourists fall toward the "casual" rather than the "dedicated" end of the spectrum.

Table 15 Purposes of Trip (1999)*

	% of Ecotourists	% of Nature Tourists	% of all Travelers
Business/Professional	6.2	7.3	31.0
Convention/Conference	0.8	0.3	4.3
Health Treatment	1.0	1.2	0.9
Leisure/Rec./Holiday	92.8	80.4	57.5
Religion/Pilgrimages	1.9	1.4	2.3
Study/Teaching	6.9	4.7	4.0
Visit Friends/Relatives	30.3	46.8	39.3
Other	1.3	1.8	1.5

*Multiple responses possible. Source: In-flight Survey

The tour operator survey asked about specific client motivations in choosing a destination. Table 16 presents the results, which indicate that the tour operator clients were most heavily motivated by the availability of high quality guides (average ranking of 1.32). The importance of tour guides was then followed by the desire for small groups, uncrowded areas, and a focus on education. The tour operators also indicated that their clientele did not seem to be nearly as concerned with relaxation, trip costs, or sports activities in comparison to a number of other trip aspects. However, there was considerable variation in the responses among the various operators, suggesting that different operators target different segments of the ecotourism market.

Table 16 Ecotourism Preferences

	Most Important	Next Most Important	Lesser Importance	Ave. Rank
Excellent Local Guides	74%	24%	3%	1.32
Small Groups	56%	29%	15%	1.59
Uncrowded Areas	56%	18%	26%	1.74
Education	35%	47%	18%	1.74
High Quality Food	29%	44%	26%	2.03
High Quality Accommodation	32%	35%	32%	2.24
Conservation	15%	38%	47%	2.56
Relaxation	9%	26%	65%	3.06
Low Cost	3%	9%	85%	3.38
Sports/Adventure	9%	21%	71%	3.41

Source: Tour Operator Survey, 2001

One of the interesting questions for the ecotourism industry is the extent to which environmentally conscious travelers will be willing to pay a premium if they are confident that sustainable ecotourism criteria are being followed by the various service providers. The tour operators provided an optimistic assessment regarding the willingness of U.S. ecotourists to pay extra for these assurances. Over two-thirds (68 percent) of the respondents believed that their clients would be willing to pay a premium. Of those that were willing to estimate what the amounts would be, about one-third believed that their clients would be willing to pay a premium of up to five percent. Almost two-thirds believed that their clients would be willing to pay between five and ten percent additional. Only one of the respondents believed that their clients would be willing to pay premiums of over ten percent to assure that sustainable ecotourism criteria were being followed.

4.3 Preferred Activities

Perhaps the single most important finding of the In-flight Survey is the extent to which U.S. ecotourists also participated in a wide variety of other activities. This suggests that most ecotourists fall more toward the "casual" than the "dedicated" end of the scale. Table 17 shows the percentage of ecotourist travelers that participated in other activities.

Table 17 Percent of U.S. Outbound Travelers Engaged in Various Leisure Activities in 1999

Leisure Activity	% Ecotourists	% All Travelers
Environmental/Eco.Excursions	100.0	4.2
Dining in Restaurants	85.4	85.2
Sholpping	82.1	75.2
Visit Small Towns	69.7	42.1
Visit Historical Places	69.6	51.0
Touring the Countryside	69.0	34.9
Cultural Heritage Sites	63.2	29.3
Sightseeing in Cities	60.3	43.0
Water Sports/Sunbathing	56.1	26.0
Visit National Parks	45.5	8.4
Ethnic Heritage Sites	38.4	12.6
Guided Tours	38.0	16.4
Art Gallery/Museum	37.4	26.7
Nightclubs/Dancing	35.4	25.0
Camping/Hiking	29.6	4.7
Concert/Play/Musical	19.8	13.8
Cruises, 1 Night +	13.7	4.4
Hunting/Fishing	13.3	4.2
Amusements/Theme Parks	12.4	9.9
Golfing/Tennis	10.9	7.2
Casinos/Gambling	7.8	7.0
Attend Sports Event	7.5	3.9
Ranch Vacations	6.9	1.8
Snow Skiing	2.2	1.5

Source: In-flight Survey

Two things are striking about the survey results. The first is that most ecotourists were engaged in multi-purpose vacations. In fact, they were more likely to engage in every single one of the potential leisure activities than the average American international tourist. These included such things as going to nightclubs and dancing or going to casinos and gambling, which would not normally be associated with ecotourism.

Table 17 indicates that the average ecotourist participated in more than ten other activities during his or her international trip. If we make the plausible assumption that an equal amount of time was spent on each activity, the In-flight Survey implies that the typical U.S. outbound ecotourist would have spent only nine percent of his or her time engaged in environmental or ecological excursions. Even more extreme, the average U.S. international tourist would have spent only 0.7 percent of his or her time in ecotourism type activities. This suggests that ecotourism, when measured in terms of the percent of time spent participating in ecotourism activities rather than simply whether it was one of the many activities engaged in, may be an even smaller portion of the market than previously indicated.

The second important finding from the survey is that ecotourists showed significant differences from the average U.S. international traveler in ways that would be expected. For example, ecotourists were more than six times as likely to go camping or hiking than the average tourist. They were five times more likely to visit national parks, three times as likely to visit ethnic heritage sites and to take ranch vacations, and twice as likely to participate in water sports and visit cultural heritage sites.

These comparisons indicate that, while U.S. ecotourists are different from the average tourist in significant aspects, they are probably not as different as the academic literature and research generally portrays them. This is probably partly because most ecotourists fall toward the "casual" versus the "dedicated" end of the scale. As a result, many of the most important and relevant policy issues are likely to involve how ecotourism principles relate to the majority of general tourists who participate only casually in ecotourism activities than to the hard-core or dedicated ecotourist.

The tour operator survey also asked about the types of activities that were important to their clients in choosing a destination. These questions were designed to narrow down the priorities among a set of ecotourism-type activities. Table 18 presents the results, which indicate ecotourist motivations as seen through the eyes of the tour operators. The survey indicates three broad categories of preferences. Wilderness and viewing wildlife clearly were the highest priority (average rankings of less than 2). These were followed by a number of intermediate priorities – birdwatching, viewing rare animals, marine and other water activities, indigenous people, and archeology (all with rankings between 2.50 and 2.76). Finally, botany and geology were viewed as much less attractive (with rankings well over 3). However, there was considerable variation in the responses among the various operators, suggesting again that different operators target different segments of the ecotourism market.

Table 18 Ecotourism Preferences Activities (Percent of respondents in each category)

	Most Important	Next Most Important	Lesser* Importance	Ave. Rank
Wildlife Viewing	53%	24%	21%	1.74
Wilderness	41%	26%	24%	1.97
Rare Species	26%	21%	59%	2.50
Archeology	21%	35%	44%	2.62
Indigenous People	18%	41%	35%	2.65
Birdwatching	21%	21%	59%	2.71
Marine/Water Activity	12%	44%	44%	2.76
Botany	3%	9%	88%	3.65
Geology	0%	6%	94%	3.91

*Includes rankings 3, 4, and 5. Source: Tour Operator Survey, 2001

4.4 Preferred Accommodations

As shown earlier in Table 16, almost one-third of the tour operators ranked high quality accommodations as being in the most important category for their clients, while another third ranked high quality accommodations in the least important categories.   While the sample size is small, there does appear to be a rough correlation between the target market (high-end, mid-level, and budget) and the relative importance of high-quality accommodations. As would be expected the operators who serve the high-end market rank high quality accommodations as being considerably more important. Almost half of these operators ranked high-quality accommodations in the most important category. This was in contrast to those serving the middle market where less than one-quarter ranked high-quality accommodations in the most important category.   Not surprisingly, the two operators who work with budget travelers ranked high-quality accommodations as less important.

Table 19 Importance of High-Quality Accommodations by Target Market (Percent of respondents in each category)

	Most Important	Next Most Important	Lesser* Importance
High-end	19%	11%	11%
Mid-level	11%	25%	17%
Budget	0%	0%	6%

*Includes rankings 3, 4, and 5. Source: Tour Operator Survey, 2001

In order to keep the questions short, the tour operator survey did not attempt to determine what types of accommodations were preferred beyond the relative importance of high quality lodging. However, an extensive phone survey of North American ecotourists (including Canadians as well as Americans) conducted in 1994 resulted in some interesting findings, which are presumably still valid today.13 That survey indicated a clear preference by ecotourists for alternative accommodations versus the standard hotels and motels preferred by most traditional travelers as shown in Table 20.

Table 20 Ecotourist Accommodations Preferences (1994)

	Ecotourists	General Tourists
Cabins	66%	14%
Lodges and Inns	60%	14%
Camping	58%	17%
Bed & Breakfasts	41%	10%
Hotels and Motels	41%	56%
Ranches	40%	1%

Source: ARA/HLA

4.5 Means of Transportation

As noted in the introduction, heavy reliance has been placed on the In-flight Survey of U.S. international outbound air travelers. By definition this excludes travel by auto, which will be important for many destinations in Canada and Northern Mexico. The author found no data on the proportion of automobile, bus, or rail crossings into Canada or Mexico from the United States that would be accounted for by ecotourists. As a result, the findings are incomplete regarding the use of automobiles or other surface transportation by outbound ecotourists from the United States to travel to their international destinations. However, once U.S. ecotourists reach their foreign destinations, they are more likely to fly, drive, or take buses between cities than the typical U.S. international traveler.

Table 21 Transportation Outside the United States (1999)*

	Eco-Tourists	Nature Tourists	All Travelers
Airline between Citiles	53%	48%	34%
Bus between Cities	22%	23%	13%
City Subway/Tram/Bus	20%	28%	19%
Company or Private Auto	24%	31%	28%
Railroad between Cities	14%	19%	17%
Motor Home/Camper	2%	1%	0.4%
Rented Auto	24%	27%	20%
Taxi/Cab/Limousine	50%	42%	48%

*Multiple responses possible. Source: In-flight Survey

4.6 Types of Information Used

The In-flight survey asks a question "how did you obtain the information used to plan your trip." As shown in Table 22, the ecotourists (and to a lesser extent, the nature tourists) showed some significant differences from the average U.S. international traveler. Perhaps most importantly, the ecotourists were more than twice as likely to use personal computers for information (36 versus 16 percent). They were four times as likely to use tour operators for information (17 versus 4 percent) and three times as likely to use travel guides (18 versus 6 percent). However, ecotourists, nature tourists and all travelers were most likely to take advantage of information provided by travel agents in obtaining the information used to plan their trips.

Table 22 Information Sources (1999)

	Eco-Tourists	Nature Tourists	All Travelers
Airline Directly	24%	26%	24%
Corporate Travel Dept.	2%	2%	10%
Personal Computer	36%	31%	16%
Friends or Relatives	22%	24%	16%
In-flight Information	2%	1%	1%
National Tourist Offices	2%	1%	0.4%
Rented Auto	4%	5%	2%
Newspapers/Magazines	8%	7%	3%
State/City Travel Office	1%	3%	2%
Tour Company	17%	10%	4%
Travel Agency	55%	53%	54%
Travel Guides	18%	14%	6%
TV/Radio	1%	1%	0.6%

Source: In-flight Survey

5. Marketing and Promotional Channels

5.1 Role and Size of Tour Operators and Travel Agents

The survey of ecotourism tour operators was intentionally oriented toward companies that emphasize ecotourism. Almost half of those sent surveys are members of The International Ecotourism Society (TIES) and therefore have a strong presumed interest in ecotourism. The remaining 62 companies that received the survey included all of the tour operators listed in the National Tour Association (NTA) directory who included ecotours among their offerings. The NTA directory included over 1200 members, so only about five percent of the U.S. tour operators even offered ecotours. In addition, the NTA members offering ecotours averaged over half a dozen other types of tours as well, indicating that most served a number of other segments beyond ecotourism. As a result, ecotourism appears to be a relatively small share of the overall business of the American tour industry. There does, however, appear to be a strong specialization in ecotourism among those operators responding to the survey, with 41 percent focusing almost exclusively (i.e., over 90% of their business) on ecotourism, as shown in Table 23. Most if not all of the exclusive ecotourism operators probably came from the TIES membership, but since some of the responses were sent in anonymously, it is not possible to confirm this.

Table 23 Share of Ecotourism in U.S. Tour Operator Offerings (Number and percent of respondents in each category)

Share of Business	Number of Operators	Percent of Operators
Less than 10%	4	12%
11-25%	3	9%
26-50%	5	15%
51-75%	5	15%
76-90%	3	9%
Over 90%	14	41%

Source: Tour Operator Survey, 2001

The U.S. tour operators were also asked to indicate the share of their ecotourism business that was accounted for by U.S. outbound, U.S. domestic, and foreign inbound ecotourists. As shown in Table 24, over a third (34 percent) of the respondents concentrated exclusively on U.S. outbound ecotourism. Moreover, outbound tour operations accounted for more than three-quarters of the business for well over half (56 percent) of the operators, indicating a high degree of specialization in the outbound segment of the industry. However, almost a quarter (22 percent) of the respondents conducted no outbound tour operations at all. Thus, despite the prevalence of outbound operators in the survey, a significant number of domestic and inbound specialists also responded to the survey. As a result, the findings from the tour operator survey should probably be interpreted as reflective of the broader U.S. industry rather than just the outbound ecotourism segment.

Table 24 Share of Inbound, Outbound, and Domestic Ecotourism Business (Percent in each category)

	100%	76%-90%	51%-75%	26%-50%	1%-25%	0%	Total
U.S. Outbound	34%	22%	3%	9%	9%	22%	100%

Source: Tour Operator Survey

The survey indicates, not surprisingly, that U.S. tour operators focus on the mid- and higher-end of the ecotourism market, where the business potential is the greatest. Table 25 indicates that a slight majority were targeting the mid-level market and almost as many were aiming at the high-end traveler. Only two of the respondents indicated a focus on the budget-level ecotourist (and one of those two also indicated that they served the mid-level and high-end of the market as well). This, of course, does not suggest that the majority of ecotourists are mid- or high-end travelers, but only that U.S. tour operators are less likely to find budget level travelers to be an attractive target market because of their unwillingness to pay for the kinds of services offered by tour operators.

Table 25 Target Markets for the U.S. Tour Operators (Number and percent of respondents in each category)

Target Market	Number of Operators*	Percent of Operators
High-end	16	42%
Mid-level	20	53%
Budget	2	5%

Note: One operator indicated all three markets and one indicated high and mid-level; Source: Tour Operator Survey, 2001

The U.S. tour operators were also asked whether the share of their business comprised by ecotourism had increased, decreased, or stayed about the same. The most common response was that the share of their business had stayed about the same over the last five years. This is not surprising in view of the large number of operators whose business already was over 90 percent ecotourism. These operators had little or no room to increase the share of their business accounted for by ecotourism.

Table 26 Share of U.S. Tour Operator Ecotourism Business over the Past Five Years (Number and percent of respondents in each category)

Share of Business	Number of Operators	Percent of Operators
Relatively Constant	22	65%
Increasing	10	29%
Decreasing	2	6%

Source: Tour Operator Survey, 2001

The tour operators were also asked whether they thought that ecotourism would be a relatively constant, increasing, or decreasing share of their business over the next five years. In this case, the respondents were more optimistic about the future than the past. As shown in Table 27, over half thought that ecotourism would be an increasing share of their business (which could be a challenge given the large portion of operators who are already almost pure ecotourism businesses). About one-third of the respondents thought that share of ecotourism in their business would stay about the same, and one-sixth thought that it would actually decline over the next five years.

Table 27 Projected Share of Tour Operator Ecotourism Business over the Next five Years (Number and percent of respondents in each category)

Share of Business	Number of Operators	Percent of Operators
Relatively Constant	11	32%
Increasing	18	53%
Decreasing	5	15%

Source: Tour Operator Survey

From all appearances, the tour operators responding to the survey are committed to ecotourism principles. Eighty-four percent of the operators indicated that they used the concept of ecotourism in promoting their company. More importantly, a large majority of the operators had specific programs to: (a) minimize adverse impacts on the environment; (b) encourage clients to contribute money or time to conservation; (c) encourage a greater understanding of the natural environment; and (d) to promote the economic well-being of local communities.

Table 28 Tour Operators commitment with sustainability: (Number and percent of respondents in each category)

Programs to:	Number of Operators	Percent of Operators
Minimize adverse environmental impacts	28	82%
Encourage contributions to conservation	25	74%
Encourage greater understanding of nature	30	88%
Promote local economic well-being	31	91%

Source: Tour Operator Survey

Examples of specific steps taken by the tour operators range from general statements of adherence to ecotourism principles to very specific steps, including:

Minimizing Environmental Impacts:

- "Our guides are specifically trained to adhere to rules and regulations that are designed to minimize negative impacts."
- "We provide onboard educational and training programs regarding ecology, observational best practices, etc."
- "We only allow guests to walk on elevated boardwalks."
- "We offer a way for customers to compensate for their greenhouse gas emissions as they relate to air travel."
- "We take $ and invest in energy saving projects (voluntary service fee passed on to customers)."
- "We hand out mugs so we don't use disposable cups."

Encouraging Contributions to Conservation:

- "We request all our clients to pay to join a local conservation group we identify – 95 percent do it."
- "We encourage donations to restoration projects."
- "We sponsor working-action trips to support conservation."
- "We support a local turtle program."

Encouraging Greater Understanding of Nature:

- "We employ premier naturalist guides."
- "All tours escorted by company multi-lingual, naturalist staff."
- "Onboard lectures by professors, other local experts, reading lists, etc."
- "Many of our guides are marine biologists and give lectures and informal presentations throughout our trips, educating our guests about the natural environment they are enjoying as well as ways to aid in its conservation."

Promoting Local Economic Well-being:

- "We strive as much as possible to utilize local nationals and locally-owned enterprises in our tours (ground operators, guides, accommodations, etc.)"
- "We provide useful materials to local schools, include students as paid guides, and buy locally."
- "We not only encourage clients to contribute to local community development efforts (through us), we also devote a portion of our profits to community projects."
- "We have created a non-profit organization to support projects."
- "We carefully select inbound operators who are trained in working with local communities. Also, we support development of village home stay programs."
- "We run a non-profit organization which sets up libraries in Nepal."

One of the uncertainties about the U.S. ecotourism market is the allocation between free and independent travelers (FITs) versus group travelers. In an effort to shed some light on this issue, the survey asked operators to estimate the percentage allocation between FITs and group travelers for their primary destinations. In addition to the usual cautions about the small sample size it appears that some of the respondents may have mis-understood the question, since three indicated that 100 percent of the visitors to their primary destinations came with tour groups. While this might be the case for a few destinations, such as Antarctica or Galapagos, it seems more likely that some of the respondents interpreted the question as applying only to their operations. The tour operators may also be somewhat biased simply because it is their business to organize group tours. As a result, the estimate by the operators that about two-thirds of the visitors to their primary destinations came with groups should be viewed with caution.

The In-flight survey presents a significantly different picture of the independent traveler. In this case U.S. outbound passengers were asked whether their trip was "part of a package." Two-thirds of the ecotourists indicated that they did not use any package services at all (i.e., that they were FITs). Despite the prevalence of FITs in the In-flight Survey it appears that ecotourists were over twice as likely to use some kind of package as the average traveler, as shown in Table 29. In addition, there appears to have been a slight increase in the percentage of ecotourists using package tours, up from 31 percent in 1996 to 33 percent in 1999. Nature travelers fall somewhere in between ecotourists and all travelers in terms of their use of package tours.

Table 29 Use of Package Tours (1999)

	Eco-Tourists	Nature Tourists	All Travelers
No	66.6%	79.0%	85.9%
Yes*	33.4%	21.0%	14.1%
Air/Lodging	21%	13%	10%
Air/Lodging/Bus	6%	4%	3%
Air/Lodging/Bus/Tour	4%	4%	2%
Air/Lodging/Rent Car	2%	1%	0.5%
Air/Lodging/Tour	9%	7%	4%
Air/Rent Car	2%	1%	1%
Guided Tour	19%	14%	7%
Cruise	6%	10%	4%
Travel Agency	55%	3%	2%

*Multiple responses possible, Source: In-flight Survey

In an effort to identify potential trends in independent versus tour travel, the survey of tour operators asked whether the operators thought that the share of independent travelers was increasing, decreasing, or staying about the same. Of the respondents answering that question (four did not venture a guess), 60 percent thought that the relative share of FITs and groups was staying about the same, while 33 percent thought that the share of FITs was increasing and only 7 percent thought that it was decreasing. These estimates suggest that, if anything, tour ecotourism operators might be playing a marginally less significant role in the future.

The tour operators indicated that travel agents were the least important marketing channel that they used (although it is interesting that one specialty cruise operator included along with its brochure an extensive list of travel agents that the company used to help market its product). Table 30 below indicates the spread of opinion about the role of travel agents, with almost two-thirds of tour operators ranking travel agents in the least important categories. The tour operators are professionals in the field and can apparently make their decisions and act independently of the travel agents.

Table 30 Relative Importance of Travel Agents to Tours Operators (Percent of respondents in each category)

	Most Important	Next Most Important	Lesser* Importance
Importance of Travel Agent	12%	24%	65%

*Includes rankings 3, 4, and 5. Source: Tour Operator Survey, 2001

The traveling public, on the other hand, still seems to need and value the services of the travel agent. Table 22 above compared the role of travel agents with other sources of information in making travel decisions. In this case, the individual ecotourists indicated that travel agents were by far the most important source of information for them, with well over half of the ecotourists relying on travel agents for information. As a result, it appears that the perception of the importance of travel agents depends very much on the vantage point, with travelers looking to them for information and tour operators believing that they play a limited role.

5.2 Direct Marketing and Online Marketing by Suppliers

Given the apparent constant, or even slightly declining role of tour operators, it would appear that suppliers would have a good opportunity for direct marketing. The survey of tour operators suggested they had widely varying views on the usefulness of online marketing. Nonetheless, as shown in Table 31, almost one-quarter ranked the Internet in the most important category, and another one-third listed it in the next most important category.

Table 31 Relative Importance of On-line Marketing (Percent of respondents in each category)

	Most Important	Next Most Important	Lesser* Importance
Internet Importance	24%	32%	44%

*Includes rankings 3, 4, and 5. Source: Tour Operator Survey, 2001

As shown in Table 32, the In-flight Survey indicates a dramatic increase in the use of personal computers for gathering information and making reservations. In 1996, only 5.5 percent of the U.S. ecotourists used the Internet for travel information. By 1999, 35.8 percent of the ecotourists were using the Internet for travel information, which was over twice the level of usage by all U.S. international travelers. However, in 1999, only 4.3 percent of the ecotourists were using the personal computer to make airline reservations, so there is still a substantial difference between information seeking and on-line booking.

Table 32 Use of the Personal Computer by U.S. Travelers (1999) (Percent of respondents in each category)

	1996 Ecotourists	1999 Ecotourists	1996 All Travelers	1999 All Travelers
For Getting Information	5.5%	35.8%	4.2%	16.0%
For Booking Tickets	0.1%	4.3%	0.4%	3.3%

Source: In-flight Survey

5.3 Role of Foreign National Tourism Offices

The tour operator survey indicated very little value added by foreign national tourism offices. Only three respondents reported that national tourism offices were useful to them in marketing ecotourism. Furthermore, one of these, whose business was half inbound and half outbound ecotourism, cited the value that they received from the Florida State Tourism Office, so it is unclear whether they also felt that they had received useful assistance from any foreign national tourism offices. The other two positive respondents noted that national tourism offices were helpful in providing good maps and information on natural attractions and in providing promotional materials and brochures.

All the other respondents indicated that foreign tourism offices were not useful to them in marketing ecotourism. One tour operator noted that "we have not used them very often, but generally find their orientation to be too mass-tourism oriented." Another operator commented that while they had not found national tourism offices useful to date, they would appreciate editorial information and educational TV programs. The participants in the focus groups concurred with the viewpoint that national tourism offices were of limited direct value. However, one noted that some of the national tourism offices helped local lodges and in-bound tour operators get media coverage which they would not otherwise be able to afford on their own. This tour operator did find that the information from local lodges and ground operators was quite useful and that the national tourism offices, therefore, played an important indirect role.

The In-flight Survey presents a mixed picture. It appears that individual ecotourists made relatively little use of information from National Government Tourism Offices for information in making decisions about where to travel, but that the percent increased slightly from 1996 to 1999. Conversely, the average American outbound air traveler made much less use of these sources of information and the percentage taking advantage of them actually declined a bit. As a result, it would appear that National Tourism Offices in countries that feature ecotourism as an important part of their product mix, should consider additional promotional and informational materials focused on ecotourism opportunities.

Table 33 Use of National Tourism Offices by Individual U.S. Travelers (1999)

	1996 Ecotourists	1999 Ecotourists	1996 All Travelers	1999 All Travelers
Using National Offices	4.1%	4.4%	1.9%	1.6%

Source: In-flight Survey

5.4 Timing Considerations

The In-flight survey indicates that ecotourists (and to a lesser extent, nature tourists) make trip decisions further in advance that the average traveler. For example, about one-quarter of the ecotourists made their decisions within one month of departure, whereas almost half of all tourists made their decisions within the last month. Conversely, almost half of the ecotourists made their decisions at least three months prior to departure, whereas less than one quarter of all tourists planned that far ahead. This indicates that ecotourism marketing decisions and supporting materials need to be prepared substantially earlier than promotional activities aimed at the general tourism market.

Table 34 Advance Trip Decisions (1999) (Percent of respondents in each category)

	Eco-Tourists	Nature Tourists	All Tourists
Same Day	-	-	0.3%
1-3 days	0.9%	2%	5%
4-7 days	3%	2%	7%
8-14 days	3%	3%	10%
15-30 days	18%	19%	24%
31-60 days	15%	19%	17%
61-90 days	10%	14%	11%
91-120 days	8%	7%	6%
121-180 days	19%	13%	9%
181 or more days	21%	19%	9%
Mean number of days	137.6	121.1	80.0

Source: In-flight Survey

5.5 Main Promotional Events in the United States

Participation in the main promotional events for travel agents and tour operators is probably not a good idea for most foreign ecotourism companies. The two travel agents who participated in the focus group said that they did not even go to the big regional meetings for the American Society of Travel Agents (ASTA) because they did not cover the ecotourism issues of interest to them. This is likely to be the case with the other travel agents that specialize in ecotourism. Similarly, the big promotional events for tour operators, such as the National Tour Association's annual Spring Meet, are so broad as to be of limited relevance to ecotourism suppliers from outside the United States.

The best opportunity for foreign suppliers to meet with U.S. tour operators and travel agents specializing in ecotourism, is the International Adventure Travel & Outdoor Sports Show (IATOS). IATOS has traditionally concentrated on the adventure segment of the market, but has always had a component dealing with ecotourism. In 2002, they will give additional prominence to ecotourism, partly because of The International Year of Ecotourism. The IATOS World Congress on Adventure & Eco Tourism will be held this year in Chicago, Illinois from February 21-24, 2002. As one of its main themes, the show will include an ecotourism conference, and eco-expo pavilion, and eco-awards. It anticipates that total attendees will include 5,000 professionals from the adventure and ecotourism travel industry, 20,000 members of the traveling public, and over 400 exhibiting organizations from more than 75 countries. For more information contact IATOS by telephone (at 877-604-2867) or by e-mail (at iatos@msemgmt.com).

5.6 Typical Promotional Tools and Information Provided

The tour operator survey indicated that word of mouth is the most important promotional tool. Brochures were the next most important promotional tool for the tour operators, followed by mailings and by the Internet. Travel agents were the least important tool for the operators. However, the averages cover a wide range of preferred promotional tools and it is dangerous to generalize too much based on the averages. For example, four operators ranked travel agents in the category of their most important promotional tools, while eight ranked them as the least important. Eight ranked catalogues in the category of most important tools, while seven other ranked them as least important. Thus, the selection among preferred promotional tools appears to vary significantly among individual tour operators, as shown in Table 35.

Table 35 Marketing Channels mentioned by Tour Operators (Percent of respondents in each category)

	Most Important	Next Most Important	Lesser* Importance	Ave. Rank
Word of Mouth	68%	24%	9%	1.42
Brochures	41%	26%	32%	1.97
Mailings	29%	38%	32%	2.21
Internet	24%	32%	44%	2.45
Catalogues	26%	24%	50%	2.79
Affinity Groups	24%	26%	68%	2.79
Advertisements	3%	29%	68%	3.27
Travel Agents	12%	24%	65%	3.29

*Includes rankings 3, 4, and 5. Source: Tour Operator Survey, 2001

The In-flight survey provides useful information on the means of booking trips for the air transportation segment of trips. Somewhat in contrast to the opinions expressed by the tour operators, travel agents are still the preferred means of booking airline trips, with well over half of ecotourists, nature tourists, and general travelers using travel agents. On the other hand, ecotourists are some what more likely to book with the airlines directly and more than three times as likely to book through tour operators, as shown in Table 36.

Table 36 Means of Booking Air Trip (1999) (Percent of respondents in each category)

	Eco-Tourists	Nature Tourists	All Tourists
Airline Directly	27%	26%	21%
Company Travel Dept.	1%	2%	10%
Personal Computer	4%	5%	3%
Travel Agent	55%	55%	59%
Travel Club	2%	2%	1%
Tour Operator	9%	6%	3%
Don't Know	1%	0.5%	1%
Other	0.9%	3%	2%

Source: In-flight Survey

Annexes

A. IN-FLIGHT SURVEY DATA FOR 1996 AND 1999

B. IN-FLIGHT SURVEY QUESTIONNAIRE

C. TOUR OPERATORS QUESTIONNAIRE

D. SELECTED CONTACTS

E. LIST OF PUBLICATIONS AND REPORTS CONSULTED

Annex A

ITA Tourism Industries

In - Flight Survey Data

January - December 1996 & 1999

U.S. Travelers to Overseas and Mexico

Data Sponsor/Administrator:
U.S. Department of commerce

Produced by: International Trade Administration **Produced for:**
CIC Research, Inc Tourism Industries Eco Tourism International
8361 Vickers Street 14th& Constitution Avenue, NW 11611 East Berry Ave.
San diego, CA 92111 Washington, D.C. 20230 Englewood, CO 80111

Survey Background

This report is based on data collected for the U.S. Department of Commerce - international Trade Administration (LTA), Tourism Industries office. The agency-sponsored research program, "The Survey of International Air Travelers", has been conducted monthly since 1983. The survey is currently available in twelve language versions, and is attached at the back of this report for your reference. For more information on Tourism Industries, visit their web site at:
http://tinet.ita.doc. gov

Visitor Definition

Many of the reports have a column titled "All Overseas". Unless otherwise specified, the definition of Overseas excludes visitors from Mexico and Canada.

Caveats in using the Data

The survey is dependent on cooperation from the airline industry, as airline participation is voluntary. Therefore special attention should be given to the page on which participating carriers are listed for the subset that has been specified for this report. General world regions for which data reliability could be affected by limited foreignflag participation include Africa, the Middle East, Caribbean and South and Central America.

Estimates of total visitor volume can be found at the end of Table 1. These estimates are based on Immigration and Naturalization Service (INS) Form 1-94 combined with the survey data.

All data presented in this report are statistical estimates, based on survey responses weighted with data from the Inmigration and Naturalization Service (INS). The estimates are subject to a certain amount of error, resulting frrom the sampling, data collection, and estimation processes. Because of the complicated nature of the sample design, sampling variability has not been calculated for those estimates. Instead, an indication of reliability is given by the number of respondents to the relevant questionnaire item (shown as the first row in each table). The reader must exercise judgement in determining the amount of confidence to place in an estimate. For example, an estimate based on 500 respondents is more reliable than one based on 25o respondents is more reliable than one based on 250 respondents. Where the number of respondents is less than 250, extra caution should be used in interpreting the results.

Country-level data, in particular should be viewed with caution. Airline participation is voluntary and can change from quarter. Therefore, if a major carrier for a particular country was unable to participate for a quarter, the data for that country may not fully represent the country's international travelers.

In 1996, Sanford International Airport, located approximately 25 miles from metro Orlando Florida, began serving the internattional market. In 1998, data collection comenced at Sanford, which primarily serves the British charter market, althouhg some German charters are also represented in the 1998 data.

Plaease be aware that these international air travelers are not directly represented in Tourism Industries' data in 1996 and 1997. Direct comparisons by markets served by Sanford may not be possible. In addition, 1996/1997 vs. 1998 comparisons of British and German leisure travelers' market shares may be affected. The 1998 data for this market, in particular, is more representative than in previous years.

Airlines and their codes to consider for Sanford intercepts are Airtours International (VZ), Britannia Airways Ltd. (BY), Leisure International (MV), Caledonian Airways (KT), Monarch Airlines (ZB), and Brritannia Airways GMBH (BN).

ITA and its contractor continue to seek global representation for greater accuracy and statistical reliability. Constant attention is paid to airline response performance to ensure the best available data for each world region.

How to use the report

Please note that tables in this report are designed to be read vertically, the data does not sum horizontally.

Some tables are multiple response. Totals on multiple response tables will often exceed 100%. An example is the International Destinations Table. Typically, international travelers visit more than one destination; therefore the column totals on the International Destinations table will exceed 100%.

The visitor volume estimates found at the end of Table 1 can be used to estimate the number of visitors for any row. This can be accomplished by multiplying thc control total times the percentage in a particular row.

U.S. Travelers to Overseas and Mexico

January - December 1996 and 1999
Produced for: **ECO Tourism International**

Airline Code

AA	AMERICAN AIRLINES		RO	VARIG
AF	AIR FRANCE		SA	SOUTH AFRICAN AIR
AM	AEROMEXICO		5K	SAS
AR	AEROLINEAS ARGENTINAS		SN	SABENA
AT	ROYAL AIR MAROC		SQ	SINGAPORE AIRLINES
AV	AVIANCA		1W	TWA
AY	FINNAIR		UA	UNITED
AZ	ALITALIA		CA	AIR CHINA
BA	BRITISH AIRWAYS		OA	OLYMPIC AIR
BW	BWIA		UP	BAHAMASAIR
CI	CHINA AIRLINES		SR	SWISSAIR
CO	CONTINENTAL AIRLINES		IB	IBERIA
DL	DELTA AIRLINES		MH	MALAYSIAN AIRLINES
GU	AVIATECA		CF	FAUCETT PERU
JL	JAPAN AIRLINES		LA	LAN CHILE
JM	AIR JAMAICA		NH	ANA
KE	KOREAN AIR		C2	AIR MICRONESIA
KU	KUWAIT AIR		GA	GARUDA INDONESIA
LH	LUFTHANSA		HP	AMERICA WEST
LR	LACSA		NZ	AIR NEW ZEALAND
MX	MEXICANA		TK	TURKISH AIRLINES
NW	NORTHWEST		OS	AUSTRIAN AIRLINES
PL	AEROPERU		LO	LOT POLISH AIRLINES
PR	PHILIPPINE AIRLINES		F1	ICELANDAIR
QF	QANTAS		VE	AVENSA
KL	KLM		SU	AEROFLOT RUSSIAN AIRLINES
US	USAIR		RO	TAROM ROMANIAN AIR TRANSPORT
LT	LTU INTERNATIONAL		BR	EVA AIRWAYS
OZ	ASIANA AIRLINES		ZB	MONARCH AIRLINES
SV	SAUDI ARABIAN AIRLINES			
VC	SERVIVENSA			

U.S. Travelers to Overseas and Mexico

January - December 1996 and 1999
Produced for: **ECO Tourism International**

State of Residence

State of Residence	Count	%	State of Residence	Count	%
Alabama	404	0.5	Mississippi	139	0.2
Alaska	134	0.2	Missouri	679	0.9
Arizona	1,297	1.8	Montana	104	0.1
Arkansas	170	0.2	Nebraska	186	0.3
California	15,556	21.1	Nevada	388	0.5
Colorado	1,546	2.1	New Hampshire	441	0.6
Connecticut	1,667	2.3	New Jersey	3,660	5.0
Delaware	174	0.2	New Mexico	281	0.4
D. Columbia	683	0.9	New York	8,663	11.7
Florida	3,539	4.8	North Carolina	1,407	1.9
Georgia	1,406	1.9	North Dakota	30	0.0
Hawaii	1,218	1.7	Ohio	1,576	2.1
Idaho	205	0.3	Oklahoma	308	0.4
Illinois	3,428	4.6	Oregon	822	1.1
Indiana	731	1.0	Pennsylvania	2,965	4.0
Iowa	351	0.5	Rhode Island	300	0.4
Kansas	338	0.5	South Caroline	523	0.7
Kentucky	337	0.5	South Dakota	55	0.1
Louisiana	411	0.6	Tennessee	581	0.8
Maine	259	0.4	Texas	3,347	4.5
Maryland	2,132	2.9	Utah	546	0.7
Massachusetts	2,761	3.7	Vermont	182	0.2
Michigan	1,260	1.7	Virginia	2,746	3.7
Minnesota	913	1.2	Washington	1,834	2.5
Wyoming	72	0.1	West Virginia	156	0.2
American Samoa	2	0.0	Wisconsin	727	1.0
Guam	23	0.0	Puerto Rico	90	0.1
North Mariana Is.	4	0.0	U.S. Virgin Is.	8	0.0
			Total Respondents	**73,765**	**100.0**

List of Tables

Additional Information

Note: In this report leisure travelers are defined as travelers who stated their main purpose of trip was either Leisure/Recreation/Holidays/Sightseeing or Visit friends/Relatives. Business travelers are defined as travelers who stated their main purpose of trip was Business/Professional or Convention/Conference/trade show.

The column definitions are as follows:

1. Survey Year 1996 US to Overseas: All U.S. travelers who visited overseas countries (including Mexico) sin 1996.

2. Survey Year 1996 Leisure env-Eco: All U.S. Leisure Travelers who visited overseas countries (including Mexico) in 1996 and stated Environmental/Ecological excursions as part of their leisure activities.

3. Survey Year 1996 Leisure Natl Prk: All U.S. Leisure Travelers who visited overseas countries (including Mexico) in 1996 and stated visiting National Parks as part of their leisure activities.

4. Survey Year 1996 Lei/NP env-Eco: All U.S. Leisure Travelers who visited overseas countries (including Mexico) in 1996 and stated Environmental/Ecological excursions and visiting National Parks as part of their leisure activities.

5. Survey Year 1996 Lei/NP Env/Cap: All U.S. Leisure Travelers who visited overseas countries (including Mexico) in 1996 and stated Environmental/Ecological excursions and Camping/Hiking as part of their leisure activities.

6. Visit Survey Year 1996 Business Env-Eco: All U.S. Business Travelers who visited overseas countries (including Mexico) in 1996 and stated. Environmental/Ecological excursions as part of their leisure activities.

7. Survey Year 1999 US to Overseas: All U.S. travelers who visited overseas countries (including Mexico) in 1999.

8. Survey Year 1999 Leisure Env-Eco: All U.S. Leisure Travelers who visited overseas countries (including Mexico) in 1999 and stated Environmental/Ecological excursions as part of their leisure activities.

9. Survey Year 1999 Leisure Matl Prk: All U.S. Leisure Travelers who visited overseas countries (including Mexico) in 1999 and stated visiting national Parks as part of their leisure activities.

10. Survey Year 1999 Lei/NP Env-Eco: All U.S. Leisure Travelers who visited overseas countries (including Mexico) in 1999 and stated Environmental/Ecological excursions and visiting National Parks as part of their leisure activities.

11. Survey Year 1999 Lei/NP Env/Camp: All U.S. Leisure Travelers who visited overseas countries (including Mexico) in 1996 and stated Environmental/Ecological excursions and Camping/Hiking as part of their leisure activities.

12. Visit Survey Year 1999 Business Env-Eco: All U.S. Business Travelers who visited overseas countries (including Mexico) in 1999 and stated Environmental/Ecologi~l excursions as part of their leisure activities.

YEAR - TO - DATE

US TRAVELERS TO OVERSEAS AND MEXICO PRODUCED FOR ECO TOURISM INTERNATIONAL JANUARY DECEMBER 1996 & 1999

Cross Tab 1 Section 1

TABLE 1 - Q2a. State/City of Residence (%)	Survey Year 1996						Survey Year 1999					
(Number of respondents)	US to Overseas	Leisure Env-Eco	Leisure Nati Prk	Lei/NP Env-Eco	Lei/NP Env/Camp	Business Env-Eco	US to Overseas	Leisure Env-Eco	Leisure Nati Prk	Lei/NP Env-Eco	Lei/NP Env/Camp	Business Env-Eco
	36,686	1.045	2,220	530	215	261	37.070	i~	2,356	519	198	213
NEW ENGLAND	6.7	5.5	4.0	4.7	5.4	8.3	8.9	9.6	7.4	9.5	4.6	8.8
Connecticut	2.1	1.0	0.8	0.7	1.0	3.8	2.5	3.1	1.7	2.0	1.1	0.4
Stamford, CT	0.5	0.4	0.3	0.4	0.9	0.7	0.4	–	0.3	0.1	–	–
Maine	0.3	0.6	0.5	1.1	–	1.1	0.5	0.9	0.4	1.1	1.8	0.2
Massachusetts	3.1	2.7	2.1	2.7	4.1	2.8	4.4	t.6	4.2	5.3	0.1	4.6
Boston	1.9	2.0	1.0	1.8	3.1	2.8	3.0	1.9	2.6	1.4	0.1	4.0
New Hampshire	0.6	0.6	0.2	–	–	0.5	0.8	0.2	0.5	0.1	–	2.2
Rhode Island	0.4	0.1	0.4	–	–	–	0.5	.06	0.3	0.7	1.6	1.5
Vermont	0.2	0.5	0.1	0.1	0.2	–	0.2	0.2	0.2	0.2	–	–
MIDDLE ATLANTIC	22.6	17.6	18.6	17.3	21.0	10.6	22.5	20.5	17.5	19.0	24.0	11.9
New Jersey	4.5	3.2	2.5	4.3	2.1	1.3	5.6	6.1	4.4	4.1	1.0	4.9
Bergen	1.1	0.2	0.3	0.2	0.2	0.1	1.2	1.6	1.0	–	–	0.3
Jersey City	0.3	0.1	0.3	0.1	0.3	–	0.6	0.3	0.6	0.3	–	–
Middlesex	0.7	0.8	0.5	1.4	0.4	0.3	0.9	0.4	0.5	0.1	–	1.1
Monmouth	0.5	–	0.1	–	–	–	0.6	1.8	0.9	2.1	–	–
Newark	1.0	0.8	0.4	0.8	1.2	0.6	1.7	1.7	0.9	1.1	0.8	1.2
New York	14.1	11.7	13.3	10.8	15.4	5.5	13.8	10.4	9.6	10.0	16.6	4.7
Albany	Q–3	0.1	0.1	0.3	0.6	–	0.3	0.7	0.2	0.4	–	0.1
Nassau	3.0	1.4	1.6	0.7	0.2	0.1	3.0	1.7	1.2	1.1	1.8	–
New York City	9.3	9.5	10.6	8.9	13.2	5.2	9.3	6.2	7.5	6.6	13.0	3.4
Rochester	0.3	0.1	0.5	0.2	–	–	0.2	–	0.1	–	–	–
Pennsylvania	4.0	2.7	2.7	2.2	3.5	3.8	3.1	4.0	3.1	4.9	6.4	2.3

Continued…

TABLE 1 - Q2a.

State/City of Residence (%)	Survey Year 1996						Survey Year 1999					
	US to Overseas	Leisure Env-Eco	Leisure Nati Prk	Lei/NP Env-Eco	Lei/NP Env/Camp	Business Env-Eco	US to Overseas	Leisure Env-Eco	Leisure Nati Prk	Lei/NP Env-Eco	Lei/NP Env/Camp	Business Env-Eco
Philadelphia	2.2	1.6	1.5	1.8	1.3	2.4	1.6	2.3	2.4	4.1	5.6	0.4
EAST NORTH CENTRAL	8.8	10.0	8.7	9.2	5.8	7.7	0.0	9.6	10.9	9.0	7.9	8.8
Illinois	3.9	4.3	4.8	4.7	3.8	1.5	4.7	2.8	–	2.5	4.8	2.2
Chicago	3.0	3.6	3.7	3.8	3.7	0.9	3.6	2.5	3.0	2.5	4.8	1.6
Indiana	0.9	0.8	0.5	1.0	–	0.8	0.9	0.7	1.8	0.7	–	1.5
Indianapolis	0.4	–	0.2	–	–	0.5	0.3	0.5	0.9	0.3	–	–
Michigan	1.2	0.5	0.9	0.3	0.5	1.6	1.8	0.8	2.0	0.9	1.1	0.9
Detroit	0.6	0.4	0.5	0.2	0.4	1.6	0.8	0.4	0.9	0.1	–	–
Ohio	1.8	2.6	1.5	0.6	1.1	0.3	1.8	4.2	2.5	3.9	1.0	2.8
Cincinnati	0.4	0.9	0.2	–	–	–	0.6	0.4	0.6	0.4	0.2	0.1
Cleveland	0.4	0.5	0.7	–	–	–	0.2	0.4	0.4	0.6	0.3	–
Columbus	0.4	0.2	0.2	–	–	–	0.4	1.8	0.7	2.4	–	1.3
Wisconsin	1.0	1.8	1.0	2.6	0.4	3.5	0.9	1.0	0.9	1.1	1.0	1.4
Milwaukee	0.3	1.3	0.7	2.4	–	–	0.3	0.1	0.2	0.1	0.2	1.3
WEST NORTH CENTRAL	2.6	1.3	1.7	0.9	1.2	1.9	2.9	3.1	3.5	2.3	3.9	0.7
Iowa	0.3	–	–	–	–	1.0	–	0.2	0.3	0.4	0.5	–
Kansas	0.4	0.1	0.2	0.2	–	–	0.5	0.1	0.7	0.2	0.4	–
Minnesota	0.9	0.4	0.7	0.5	0.8	0.5	1.0	0.7	1.6	1.1	2.0	0.7
Minn./St. Paul	0.8	0.4	0.6	0.3	0.5	0.2	0.8	0.5	1.4	0.8	1.8	0.7
Missouri	0.6	0.7	0.4	0.2	0.2	0.3	0.8	1.9	0.6	0.5	0.8	–
St. Louis	0.3	0.6	0.2	–	0.1	0.1	0.4	0.9	0.3	0.2	–	–
Nebraska	0.3	–	0.1	–	0.1	–	0.3	–	0.3	0.1	–	–
North Dakota	0.1	–	0.2	–	–	–	–	–	–	0.1	0.1	–
South Dakota	0.1	–	–	–	–	–	–	–	–	–	–	–

Continued....

TABLE 1 - Q2a.

State/City of Residence (%)	Survey Year 1996						Survey Year 1999					
	US to Overseas	Leisure Env-Eco	Leisure Nati Prk	Lei/NP Env-Eco	Lei/NP Env/Camp	Business Env-Eco	US to Overseas	Leisure Env-Eco	Leisure Nati Prk	Lei/NP Env-Eco	Lei/NP Env/Camp	Business Env-Eco
SOUTH ATLANTIC	20.1	21.8	22.3	23.8	11.9	32.0	15.8	13.9	11.5	11.1	6.6	26.3
Delaware	0.2	0.2	0.6	0.3	0.7	0.2	0.2	0.2	0.1	0.3	–	–
Dist. of Columbia	1.0	1.4	0.7	1.4	–	3.2	0.5	0.1	0.2	0.2	0.2	1.4
DC Metro Area	4.6	3.4	5.1	2.6	–	11.7	3.1	1.7	2.0	2.4	2.1	11.0
Florida	7.9	9.7	8.8	12.1	3.3	16.7	6.9	6.8	4.9	5.4	1.3	3.3
Ft. Lauderdale	1.3	1.2	1.1	1.7	–	0.9	0.8	0.3	0.6	0.4	–	0.2
Jacksonville	0.3	0.1	0.3	0.1	–	–	0.1	0.4	0.1	0.1	0.2	–
Miami	3.4	1.5	3.3	2.6	1.0	8.9	3.0	3.0	2.3	2.0	0.5	0.1
Orlando	0.4	1.1	0.6	1.1	0.8	0.9	0.3	0.4	0.2	–	–	–
Tampa/St. Petersburg	0.7	0.4	0.3	–	0.1	3.5	0.5	0.3	0.5	0.6	–	0.6
West Palm Beach	0.6	0.6	0.4	0.6	1.2	–	0.5	0.9	0.4	0.2	–	2.4
Georgia	2.2	1.1	0.9	0.9	–	0.3	1.7	0.4	1.2	0.7	1.5	2.8
Atlanta	1.6	0.9	0.8	0.8	–	0.3	1.4	.2	1.0	0.3	0.5	1.4
Maryland	2.8	1.7	3.9	0.5	0.1	4.6	1.7	1.2	1.0	0.5	0.1	8.9
Baltimore	1.0	0.5	1.5	0.2	–	0.2	0.6	1.0	0.3	0.2	–	6.3
North Carolina	1.8	2.9	2.8	4.4	1.6	0.7	1.5	0.9	1.3	0.4	0.6	0.3
Charlotte	0.5	–	0.6	–	–	–	0.3	0.4	0.1	0.1	–	0.1
Raleigh-Durham	0.5	1.0	0.6	1.4	0.5	0.5	0.4	0.4	0.2	0.2	0.4	–
South Carolina	0.8	1.1	0.4	–	0.1	0.3	0.5	1.1	0.7	0.2	0.1	2.4
Virginia	3.3	3.5	4.1	4.0	5.8	6.1	2.5	2.6	2.0	3.5	2.9	7.2
Norfolk	0.4	1.9	0.9	2.4	5.5	0.6	0.3	0.4	0.4	0.7	0.4	0.1
Richmond	0.4	0.3	0.3	0.6	–	0.1	0.3	0.4	0.2	–	–	–
West Virginia	0.1	0.2	–	0.1	0.3	–	0.2	0.6	–	–	–	–
EAST SOUTH CENTRAL	2.1	3.4	2.0	2.5	3.8	1.1	1.8	1.1	2.2	2.2	4.5	3.5
Alabama	0.7	0.8	0.5	0.6	0.3	0.5	–	–	–	0.3	0.2	0.1

Continued....

TABLE 1 - Q2a.

State/City of Residence (%)	Survey Year 1996						Survey Year 1999					
	US to Overseas	Leisure Env-Eco	Leisure Nati P'k	Lei/NP Env-Eco	Lei/NP Env/Camp	Business Env-Eco	US to Overseas	Leisure Env-Eco	Leisure Nati Prk	Lei/NP Env-Eco	Lei/NP Env/Camp	Business Env-Eco
Kentucky	0.5	0.7	1.0	1.4	3.5	0.1	0.3	–	0.5	–	–	1.3
Mississippi	0.2	0.2	0.1	0.1	–	0.4	0.1	–	–	–	–	0.4
Tennessee	0.7	1.7	0.3	0.5	–	–	0.8	0.9	0.8	1.8	4.3	1.8
Memphis	0.1	0.1	–	–	–	–	0.2	3.0	0.2	–	–	0.8
Nashville	0.3	0.5	–	–	–	–	0.3	0.5	0.3	1.0	2.5	1.1
WEST SOUTH CENTRAL	6.1	6.1	4.9	5.9	8.1	3.4	7.9	5.9	6.4	6.5	4.6	2.5
Arkansas	0.2	0.5	0.5	1.1	2.7	–	0.3	0.1	0.2	0.2	0.4	0.3
Louisiana	0.6	0.5	0.3	0.2	0.5	–	0.5	0.4	0.4	0.7	–	–
New Orleans	0.3	0.1	0.2	–	–	–	0.2	0.1	0.2	–	–	–
Oklahoma	0.3	0.1	0.3	0.2	0.4	0.9	0.7	0.1	0.4	0.1	0.1	–
Texas	4.9	5.0	3.8	4.4	4.4	2.5	6.4	5.3	5.4	5.5	4.1	2.2
Austin	0.4	1.6	0.8	0.1	–	0.7	0.3	0.3	0.1	–	–	0.1
Dallas	1.2	1.0	0.7	0.8	0.4	–	1.8	0.5	1.4	0.6	0.2	0.6
Ft. Worth	0.3	0.5	0.3	1.0	2.5	–	0.6	–	0.1	–	–	–
Houston	1.6	0.9	1.3	1.2	0.1	1.7	2.3	3.3	2.9	4.4	3.8	1.4
MOUNTAIN	6.2	7.4	5.6	6.4	5.3	10.4	5.9	7.6	9.5	6.2	6.7	8.0
Arizona	2.1	2.4	2.1	2.6	0.2	3.0	1.7	1.4	1.9	1.7	1.7	3.2
Phoenix	1.3	1.5	1.3	1.2	–	2.2	1.2	0.6	1.1	0.1	–	0.6
Tucson	0.6	0.3	0.3	0.1	–	–	0.3	0.4	0.5	0.8	1.5	1.7
Colorado	2.0	2.9	2.1	2.2	3.0	2.6	2.0	4.2	4.5	2.1	3.9	3.4
Boulder	0.2	0.1	0.3	0.1	0.3	–	0.3	1.7	0.9	0.6	1.3	1.3
Denver	1.2	1.7	1.0	1.4	1.9	1.3	1.1	1.1	2.5	0.6	0.4	0.6
Idaho	0.3	0.2	0.2	0.3	0.7	–	0.4	0.5	1.2	0.8	–	–
Montana	0.2	–	0.2	–	–	0.6	0.1	0.1	0.1	0.1	0.3	–

Continued...

TABLE 1 - Q2a.

State/City of Residence (%)	Survey Year 1996						Survey Year 1999					
	US to Overseas	Leisure Env-Eco	Leisure Nati Prk	Lei/NP Env-Eco	Lei/NP Env/Camp	Business Env-Eco	US to Overseas	Leisure Env-Eco	Leisure Nati Prk	Lei/NP Env-Eco	Lei/NP Env/Camp	Business Env-Eco
Nevada	0.4	0.4	0.2	0.1	0.1	1.1	0.6	0.3	0.4	0.2	0.3	0.7
Las Vegas	0.3	0.2	0.1	0.1	0.1	0.3	0.4	0.3	0.2	0.1	0.3	0.1
New Mexico	0.3	0.5	0.3	0.4	–	0.8	0.5	0.5	0.3	0.3	0.4	0.7
Utah	0.7	0.6	0.3	0.3	–	0.8	0.7	0.4	1.0	0.7	–	–
Salt Lake City	0.5	0.4	0.1	–	–	–	0.5	0.3	0.9	0.5	–	–
Wyoming	0.1	0.4	0.2	0.5	1.2	1.5	0.1	0.1	0.2	0.3	–	–
PACIFIC	23.5	25.1	29.3	25.9	33.4	23.3	23.0	27.9	29.5	33.0	35.4	20.3
Alaska	0.2	0.6	0.6	0.5	1.3	0.9	–	0.3	0.3	0.7	1.7	0.2
California	19.4	19.6	24.5	22.1	25.9	16.6	19.7	23.1	23.8	26.7	25.5	13.3
Anaheim	1.6	1.1	2.3	0.9	1.5	1.2	1.7	2.2	1.8	3.3	2.5	–
Los Angeles	6.4	5.5	6.1	5.3	5.5	3.4	4.8	4.9	5.2	6.1	3.4	3.7
Oakland	1.5	0.8	2.9	0.8	0.6	0.2	2.0	1.7	2.0	1.6	2.0	1.5
Riverside/San Bern.	0.8	0.8	0.8	0.3	0.7	0.6	0.8	0.6	0.8	1.2	2.6	–
Sacramento	0.7	1.7	1.5	3.2	4.9	0.8	0.6	0.5	0.6	0.7	0.6	–
San Diego	1.4	2.1	2.2	2.1	1.8	1.7	2.0	3.9	2.5	2.4	2.4	0.5
San Francisco	2.3	3.5	3.3	4.3	5.8	1.8	2.6	3.0	4.5	5.0	2.5	1.7
San Jose	2.0	1.6	2.2	1.8	1.3	1.0	2.7	1.1	3.2	1.9	1.0	0.8
Santa Barbara	0.4	–	0.3	–	–	–	0.2	0.3	0.2	0.3	–	–
Oregon	1.5	2.0	1.8	2.0	4.9	2.8	0.9	2.0	2.6	1.8	1.6	3.0
Portland	0.9	1.5	1.3	2.0	4.9	–	0.6	1.4	1.7	0.6	0.9	2.2
Washington	2.4	2.8	2.5	1.3	1.2	3.0	2.1	2.6	2.7	3.8	6.6	3.8
Seattle	1.5	1.6	1.5	1.0	0.5	1.5	1.5	2.2	1.5	3.2	6.4	3.7

Continued...

TABLE 1 - Q2a. State/City of Residence (%)	Survey Year 1996						Survey Year 1999					
	US to Overseas	Leisure Env-Eco	Leisure Nati Prk	Lei/NP Env-Eco	Lei/NP Env/Camp	Business Env-Eco	US to Overseas	Leisure Env-Eco	Leisure Nati Prk	Lei/NP Env-Eco	Lei/NP Env/Camp	Business Env-Eco
PACIFIC ISLANDS	1.0	1.6	2.2	2.8	4.3	1.3	1.0	0.9	1.7	1.3	1.9	6.3
Guam	0.1	–	–	–	–	–	–	–	–	–	–	–
Hawaiian Islands	0.9	1.6	2.2	2.8	4.3	1.3	1.0	0.9	1.7	1.3	1.9	6.3
Maui	0.1	0.7	0.5	1.4	2.3	–	0.1	–	0.2	–	–	–
Oahu/Honolulu	0.7	0.8	1.5	1.4	2.0	1.3	0.8	0.2	1.1	0.2	0.2	4.0
American Samoa	–	–	–	–	–	–	–	–	–	–	–	–
N. Mariana Is.	–	–	–	–	–	–	–	–	–	–	–	–
ATLANTIC ISLANDS	0.1	0.3	0.7	0.6	–	–	0.2	–	0.5	–	–	2.9
Puerto Rico	0.1	0.3	0.7	0.6	–	–	0.2	–	0.5	–	–	2.9
U.S. Virgin Is.	–	–	–	–	–	–	–	–	–	–	–	–
EXPANDED ESTIMATES IN 0005 FOR COLUMN BANNER POINTS	(23,779)	(880)	(1,641)	(404)	(166)	(143)	(29,395)	(999)	(1,969)	(441)	(176)	(147)

YEAR - TO - DATE

US TRAVELERS TO OVERSEAS AND MEXICO
PRODUCED FOR ECO TOURISM INTERNATIONAL
JANUARY DECEMBER 1996 & 1999

Cross Tab 1
Section 2

TABLE 2

Advance Trip Decision (%)	Survey Year 1996						Survey Year 1999					
	US to Overseas	Leisure Env-Eco	Leisure Nati Prk	Lei/NP Env-Eco	Lei/NP Env/Camp	Business Env-Eco	US to Overseas	Leisure Env-Eco	Leisure Nati Prk	Lei/NP Env-Eco	Lei/NP Env/Camp	Business Env-Eco
(Number of respondents)	34,926	1.011	2.140	513	210	255	35.286	1.000	2.257	502	191	208
Same Day	0.4	0.1	0.1	–	–	–	0.3	–	–	–	–	–
1 - 3 Days	6.0	1.3	1.7	0.8	–	11.4	5.2	0.9	2.3	–	–	1.7
4 - 7 Days	8.2	2.8	3.1	1.9	1.8	9.4	7.5	3.3	2.4	2.7	–	7.9
8 - 14 Days	10.1	5.1	5.3	3.6	1.9	8.4	10.1	3.3	3.5	2.6	1.8	7.9
15 - 30 Days	23.4	19.8	17.0	15.9	16.0	30.8	24.0	18.1	19.6	15.2	23.9	30.8
31 - 60 Days	18.2	18.3	21.4	22.9	24.2	10.9	17.1	15.1	18.9	19.7	20.5	19.2
61 - 90 Days	11.6	15.5	15.5	14.9	21.6	8.9	11.4	10.5	13.8	10.6	11.4	15.7
91 - 120 Days	6.0	10.6	10.4	14.7	10.7	6.1	5.9	8.5	7.6	8.8	10.8	7.4
121 - 180 Days	9.1	15.5	14.4	15.3	13.9	8.2	9.1	18.9	12.8	14.4	9.9	3.6
181 or More Days	7.0	11.0	11.1	9.9	10.0	5.8	9.4	21.3	19.0	26.1	21.7	5.8
Mean No. of Days	73.2	103.7	105.4	106.5	107.0	63.5	80.0	137.6	121.1	149.6	130.9	71.5
Median No. of Days	42.0	90.0	90.0	90.0	90.0	30.0	45.0	90.0	90.0	90.0	90.0	42.0

YEAR - TO - DATE

**Cross Tab 1
Section 2**

US TRAVELERS TO OVERSEAS AND MEXICO
PRODUCED FOR ECO TOURISM INTERNATIONAL
JANUARY DECEMBER 1996 & 1999

TABLE 3 - Q7b	Survey Year 1996						Survey Year 1999					
Advance Airline Reservation (%)	US to Overseas	Leisure Env-Eco	Leisure Nati Prk	Lei/NP Env-Eco	Lei/NP Env/Camp	Business Env-Eco	US to Overseas	Leisure Env-Eco	Leisure Nati Prk	Lei/NP Env-Eco	Lei/NP Env/Camp	Business Env-Eco
(Number of respondents)	33.600	970	2,060	497	203	245	33.865	974	2,182	492	191	206
Same Day	0.9	0.9	0.5	0.7	–	–	0.9	1.0	0.8	1.8	–	0.1
1 - 3 Days	9.4	3.0	3.4	1.1	0.8	20.9	8.1	2.1	3.9	0.5	0.6	2.3
4 - 7 Days	11.8	3.0	5.8	2.4	3.2	14.5	10.4	5.6	2.6	2.8	2.4	10.9
8 - 14 Days	12.4	7.2	8.3	6.1	4.0	7.6	12.6	6.1	9.4	7.0	9.7	20.4
15 - 30 Days	28.6	35.0	28.5	37.3	44.9	33.5	27.5	22.8	23.0	19.0	24.4	31.8
31 - 60 Days	18.0	18.9	23.4	23.5	17.8	13.8	17.6	19.1	22.8	22.2	19.3	23.5
61 - 90 Days	8.8	12.8	12.1	12.4	12.6	7.0	9.2	13.0	12.8	14.1	21.0	6.9
91 - 120 Days	4.2	8.3	7.1	5.7	4.3	1.2	4.6	8.2	6.4	9.4	10.1	1.6
121 - 180 Days	4.4	8.9	8.2	8.6	10.3	1.3	5	14.3	10.9	14.6	8.8	1.5
181 or More Days	1.4	2.1	2.7	2.3	2.1	0.2	3.0	–	7.3	8.7	3.9	0.9
Mean No. of Days	42.8	62.8	61.0	61.8	62.0	28.2	51.1	84.6	77.4	91.8	72.1	36.5
Median No. of Days	30.0	38.0	42.0	45.0	30.0	20.0	30.0	60.0	60.0	60.0	60.0	25.0

YEAR - TO - DATE

Cross Tab 1
Section 2

US TRAVELERS TO OVERSEAS AND MEXICO
PRODUCED FOR ECO TOURISM INTERNATIONAL
JANUARY DECEMBER 1996 & 1999

TABLE 4 - Q8	Survey Year 1996						Survey Year 1999					
Means of Booking Air Trip (%)	US to Overseas	Leisure Env-Eco	Leisure Nati Prk	Lei/NP Env-Eco	Lei/NP Env/Camp	Business Env-Eco	US to Overseas	Leisure Env-Eco	Leisure Nati Prk	Lei/NP Env-Eco	Lei/NP Env/Camp	Business Env-Eco
(Number of Respondents)	35.957	1,024	2,183	518	209	258	36.359	1007	2.307	507	195	212
Airline Directly	17.7	18.7	21.1	19.9	20.3	20.1	20.9	26.7	26.5	31.6	33.1	26.4
Company Travel Dept.	9.4	4.1	2.8	6.9	8.4	17.0	9.6	1.3	1.9	0.7	0.4	16.3
Personal computer	0.4	0.1	0.3	0.1	–	–	3.3	4.3	5.3	5.6	3.1	3.4
Travel Agent	64.9	57.9	64.8	54.3	49.0	56.2	58.9	54.7	55.3	49.0	57.4	43.5
Travel Club	1.3	1.9	1.4	1.7	2.2	0.4	1.2	1.7	1.6	2.2	2.4	–
Tour Operator	3.6	14.2	6.8	14.4	15.2	3.0	3.0	9.4	5.8	10.0	1.9	3.7
Don't Know	0.8	1.1	0.9	1.7	4.0	0.6	1.0	1.0	0.5	0.1	–	4.5
Other	1.9	2.1	1.9	1.1	0.8	2.7	2.1	0.9	3.0	0.9	1.7	2.2

YEAR - TO - DATE

**Cross Tab 1
Section 2**

US TRAVELERS TO OVERSEAS AND MEXICO
PRODUCED FOR ECO TOURISM INTERNATIONAL
JANUARY DECEMBER 1996 & 1999

TABLE 5 - Q6

Information Sources* (%)	Survey Year 1996						Survey Year 1999					
	US to Overseas	Leisure Env-Eco	Leisure Nati Prk	Lei/NP Env-Eco	Lei/NP Env/Camp	Business Env-Eco	US to Overseas	Leisure Env-Eco	Leisure Nati Prk	Lei/NP Env-Eco	Lei/NP Env/Camp	Business Env-Eco
(Number of Respondents)	36.125	1.034	2.200	524	212	257	36,521	1,030	2,333	518	198	212
Airline Directly	21.1	19.2	23.8	20.2	19.2	17.9	23.6	24.5	25.5	32.2	35.3	31.8
Corporate Travel Dept.	9.3	2.2	1.8	2.3	3.9	14.8	9.5	1.8	1.6	1.6	1.5	11.4
Personal computer	4.2	5.5	6.7	7.1	8.8	6.0	16.0	35.8	31.0	44.3	59.8	37.4
Friends or Relatives	16.6	25.4	29.2	28.3	32.8	12.4	15.7	22.3	24.3	30.6	38.6	11.4
In-flight Info. Systems	0.6	0.5	1.1	0.3	0.5	1.0	0.8	1.5	1.4	1.8	1.0	1.5
Nat') Govt. Tourist Ofc.	1.9	4.1	4.3	5.8	5.1	5.2	1.6	4.4	4.6	7.5	12.6	4.1
Newspapers/Magazines	4.2	8.8	7.5	11.6	12.2	4.2	3.2	7.8	7.4	9.5	16.6	2.9
State / City Travel Ofc.	2.5	3.5	4.1	4.9	9.4	1.4	2.3	1.3	3.4	2.2	1.6	1.5
Tour Company	5.0	19.4	11.1	21.2	24.8	5.5	4.2	17.1	10.2	20.6	15.3	7.8
Travel Agency	61.5	60.2	62.3	54.2	47.0	56.0	54.5	55.5	53.7	51.9	60.8	54.2
Travel Guides	6.7	12.7	13.3	16.9	23.3	9.5	6.0	17.6	14.4	22.0	25.3	9.0
TV / Radio	0.9	0.8	2.2	0.8	0.8	–	0.6	1.4	1.3	1.8	2.9	0.5

* Multiple Response.

YEAR - TO - DATE

**Cross Tab 1
Section 2**

US TRAVELERS TO OVERSEAS AND MEXICO
PRODUCED FOR ECO TOURISM INTERNATIONAL
JANUARY DECEMBER 1996 & 1999

TABLE 6 - QiSa Use of Package (%)	Survey Year 1996						Survey Year 1999					
	US to Overseas	Leisure Env-Eco	Leisure Nati Prk	Lei/NP Env-Eco	Lei/NP Env/Camp	Business Env-Eco	US to Overseas	Leisure Env-Eco	Leisure Nati Prk	Lei/NP Env-Eco	Lei/NP Env/Camp	Business Env-Eco
(Number of Respondents)	35,126	1,027	2,183	525	212	258	35,462	1,025	2,328	517	197	211
Yes	15.2	31.0	21.9	30.4	26.2	5.0	14.1	33.4	21.0	31.6	27.2	6.5
(Yes, with any package component plus):												
Air / Lodging	11.4	23.0	15.4	23.3	18.8	2.6	9.6	21.0	13.0	17.7	14.5	5.1
Air / Lodging / Bus	4.0	10.1	5.8	8.4	8.0	2.3	3.3	5.5	4.4	3.4	1.4	1.9
Air / Lodging / Bus / Tour	2.4	7.3	4.5	5.8	4.0	1.7	2.0	3.5	4.0	2.9	1.3	1.9
Air / Lodging / Rent Car	0.5	1.6	2.0	2.1	3.0	–	0.5	1.5	1.2	2.0	2.6	0.1
Air / Lodging / Tour	4.5	13.5	8.7	15.3	13.6	1.9	3.7	8.6	7.6	11.0	9.0	4.2
Air / Rent Car	0.7	1.7	2.3	2.3	3.0	–	0.8	1.5	1.3	2.1	2.8	0.9
Guided Tour	7.0	20.0	14.1	22.2	20.9	3.1	6.8	19.3	14.2	23.0	21.2	4.5
Cruise	2.2	9.9	4.1	6.3	2.0	1.8	1.7	6.4	3.4	5.4	2.5	2.3
No	84.8	69.0	78.1	69.6	73.8	95.0	85.9	66.6	79.0	68.4	72.8	93.5

* Multiple Response. Includes all package combinations. Guided Tour includes both escort and commercial tours.

YEAR - TO - DATE

Cross Tab 1
Section 2

US TRAVELERS TO OVERSEAS AND MEXICO
PRODUCED FOR ECO TOURISM INTERNATIONAL
JANUARY DECEMBER 1996 & 1999

TABLE 7 - 09	Survey Year 1996						Survey Year 1999					
Pre Booked Lodging (%)	US to Overseas	Leisure Env-Eco	Leisure Nati Prk	Lei/NP Env-Eco	Lei/NP Env/Camp	Business Env-Eco	US to Overseas	Leisure Env-Eco	Leisure Nati Prk	Lei/NP Env-Eco	Lei/NP Env/Camp	Business Env-Eco
(Number of Respondents)	35.828	1,035	2,176	525	212	260	36.167	1,024	2.322	515	198	212
Yes, Booked by*	59.5	67.0	52.7	64.8	61.2	66.3	60.0	68.4	55.4	67.9	67.7	73.4
Airline Staff	1.1	0.9	1.0	0.6	–	2.9	1.1	0.4	0.9	0.9	0.5	–
Business Associate	6.5	1.4	1.0	2.5	0.2	14.1	5.4	0.1	0.3	–	–	16.8
Company Travel Dept.	8.1	2.2	2.1	3.4	4.9	17.8	8.6	3.1	1.8	1.0	0.4	17.9
Friend or Relative	4.1	8.0	6.1	8.2	6.3	2.0	4.6	5.0	4.4	4.3	7.0	0.8
Hotel/Motel Directly	7.5	10.0	8.8	10.0	14.0	11.0	9.2	15.7	14.0	20.6	18.3	9.8
Tour Operator	5.0	17.3	10.8	19.3	18.3	3.3	4.3	14.6	9.7	17.4	12.2	2.9
Travel Agent	27.7	28.6	25.6	24.6	19.0	19.4	26.4	31.7	26.4	30.3	38.5	21.5
Other	3.9	3.4	2.6	1.0	0.1	6.9	4.8	7.2	6.1	9.7	12.6	11.6
No	40.5	33.0	47.3	35.2	38.8	33.7	40.0	31.6	44.6	32.1	32.3	26.6

* Multiple Response. Percentages based on total number of respondents.

YEAR - TO - DATE

Cross Tab 1
Section 3

US TRAVELERS TO OVERSEAS AND MEXICO
PRODUCED FOR ECO TOURISM INTERNATIONAL
JANUARY DECEMBER 1996 & 1999

TABLE 8 - 011

Travel Companions* (%)	Survey Year 1996						Survey Year 1999					
	US to Overseas	Leisure Env-Eco	Leisure Nati Prk	Lei/NP Env-Eco	Lei/NP Env/Camp	Business Env-Eco	US to Overseas	Leisure Env-Eco	Leisure Nati Prk	Lei/NP Env-Eco	Lei/NP Env/Camp	Business Env-Eco
(Number of Respondents)	35,39	1,037	2,189	525	213	251	35,618	1,016	2,305	509	195	209
Business Associates	8.3	1.2	0.6	0.2	0.3	17.9	6.7	0.8	0.3	0.2	–	10.3
Family/Relative	21.1	23.8	30.0	20.1	17.7	4.1	21.8	28.0	27.9	27.0	33.2	11.3
Friends	12.3	20.6	17.0	23.8	29.5	6.8	12.2	18.1	17.3	18.3	20.4	11.6
Spouse	29.5	43.7	40.2	41.1	33.4	17.2	29.4	48.7	42.3	49.0	48.0	31.4
Tour Group	3.0	7.1	4.4	8.1	6.6	1.6	2.3	3.3	2.7	2.7	3.0	2.6
Traveling Alone	37.9	24.0	24.6	23.8	27.2	59.9	39.4	21.5	25.8	19.9	21.2	47.1

* Multiple Response.

YEAR - TO - DATE

US TRAVELERS TO OVERSEAS AND MEXICO
PRODUCED FOR ECO TOURISM INTERNATIONAL
JANUARY DECEMBER 1996 & 1999

TABLE 9 - 012	Survey Year 1996						Survey Year 1999					
Travel Party Size (%)	US to Overseas	Leisure Env-Eco	Leisure Nati Prk	Lei/NP Env-Eco	Lei/NP Env/Camp	Business Env-Eco	US to Overseas	Leisure Env-Eco	Leisure Nati Prk	Lei/NP Env-Eco	Lei/NP Env/Camp	Business Env-Eco
(Number of Respondents)	36,319	1,043	2,214	529	215	261	36,653	1,029	2,348	518	197	213
Adults Only	93.3	91.8	87.8	93.1	95.0	97.4	93.3	90.4	90.2	92.3	90.9	96.7
Adults and Children	6.7	8.2	12.2	6.9	5.0	2.6	6.7	9.6	9.8	7.7	9.1	3.3
Mean Total Party Size	1.6	1.8	1.8	1.8	1.7	1.3	1.5	.9	1.8	1.9	2.0	1.4
Median Total Party Size	1.0	2.0	2.0	2.0	2.0	1.0	1.0	2.0	2.0	2.0	2.0	1.0
Adults Only												
(Number of Respondents)	33,100	936	1,938	481	197	252	33,300	905	2,051	459	173	205
One	68.4	49.6	53.6	48.5	52.6	82.5	69.8	46.8	54.4	43.1	45.3	75.2
Two	26.7	45.1	40.8	46.1	43.3	15.9	25.9	46.7	39.9	49.0	42.7	23.5
Three	2.4	2.0	2.4	1.0	0.5	0.4	2.2	3.8	3.0	5.1	10.1	0.5
Four or More	2.4	3.4	3.1	4.4	3.6	1.1	2.1	2.6	2.7	2.7	1.9	0.8
Mean Adult Party Size	1.4	1.6	1.6	1.7	1.6	1.3	1.4	1.7	1.6	1.7	1.7	1.3
Median Adult Party Size	1.0	2.0	1.0	2.0	1.0	1.0	1.0	2.0	1.0	2.0	2.0	1.0
Adults and Children												
(Number of Respondents)	3,219	107	276	48	18	9	3,353	124	297	59	24	8
Mean Party Size	3.4	3.7	3.3	3.6	3.7	2.7	3.5	4.0	3.4	3.8	4.0	3.6
Median Party Size	3.0	3.0	3.0	4.0	3.0	2.0	3.0	4.0	3.0	4.0	4.0	4.0

YEAR - TO - DATE

Cross Tab 1
Section 3

US TRAVELERS TO OVERSEAS AND MEXICO
PRODUCED FOR ECO TOURISM INTERNATIONAL
JANUARY DECEMBER 1996 & 1999

TABLE 10

QiDa. Main Purpose of Trip (%)	Survey Year 1996						Survey Year 1999					
	US to Overseas	Leisure Env-Eco	Leisure Nati Prk	Lei/NP Env-Eco	Lei/NP Env/Camp	Business Env-Eco	US to Overseas	Leisure Env-Eco	Leisure Nati Prk	Lei/NP Env-Eco	Lei/NP Env/Camp	Business Env-Eco
(Number of Respondents)	34.943	1.045	2.220	530	215	261	35.387	1,032	2.356	519	198	213
Business / Professional	29.2	–	–	–	–	87.4	26.5	–	–	–	–	85.9
Convention / Conference	2.6	–	–	–	–	12.6	2.5	–	–	–	–	14.1
Health Treatment	0.3	–	–	–	–	–	0.3	–	–	–	–	–
Leisure / Rec. / Holidays	38.6	76.8	64.9	75.1	72.6	–	40.9	81.8	64.3	81.3	81.6	–
Religion / Pilgrimages	1.6	–	–	–	–	–	1.2	–	–	–	–	–
Study / Teaching	1.9	–	–	–	–	–	1.6	–	–	–	–	–
Visit Friends / Relatives	24.9	23.2	35.1	24.9	27.4	–	26.6	18.2	35.7	18.7	18.4	–
Other	1.0	–	–	–	–	–	0.5	–	–	–	–	–

YEAR - TO - DATE

US TRAVELERS TO OVERSEAS AND MEXICO PRODUCED FOR ECO TOURISM INTERNATIONAL JANUARY DECEMBER 1996 & 1999

TABLE 11

Qiob. Purpose of Trip* (%)	Survey Year 1996						Survey Year 1999					
	US to Overseas	Leisure Env-Eco	Leisure Nati Prk	Lei/NP Env-Eco	Lei/NP Env/Camp	Business Env-Eco	US to Overseas	Leisure Env-Eco	Leisure Nati Prk	Lei/NP Env-Eco	Lei/NP Env/Camp	Business Env-Eco
(Number of Respondents)	34,469	1.045	2.220	530	215	261	36,826	1.032	2.356	519	198	213
Business / Professional	34.8	7.0	7.5	7.3	13.1	92.2	31.0	6.2	7.3	7.5	9.5	88.7
Convention / Conference	4.4	0.3	0.3	0.4	0.1	20.1	4.3	0.8	0.3	–	–	20.4
Health Treatment	1.2	1.7	1.2	1.1	2.6	0.9	0.9	1.0	1.2	0.1	0.2	0.4
Leisure / Rec. / Holidays	55.6	89.9	82.5	88.8	82.4	38.4	57.5	92.8	80.4	95.3	96.3	50.8
Religion / Pilgrimages	2.8	0.9	1.5	1.1	1.4	1.0	2.3	1.9	1.4	1.1	2.0	–
Study / Teaching	4.7	4.9	3.9	4.9	2.4	7.7	4.0	6.9	4.7	7.1	4.2	10.6
Visit Friends / Relatives	37.8	35.5	49.0	37.9	40.9	18.6	39.3	30.3	46.8	30.1	31.4	22.6
Other	2.5	2.2	0.9	1.4	1.8	7.5	1.5	1.3	1.8	1.2	2.2	3.4
Net Purposes of Trip:												
Business & Convention	36.8	7.2	7.8	7.6	13.1	100.0	33.2	7.0	7.5	7.5	9.5	100.0
Leisure & VFR	76.8	100.0	100.0	100.0	100.0	47.9	79.6	100.0	100.0	100.0	100.0	62.0

* Multiple Response, includes both main and secondary trip purposes

YEAR - TO - DATE

Cross Tab 1
Section 3

US TRAVELERS TO OVERSEAS AND MEXICO
PRODUCED FOR ECO TOURISM INTERNATIONAL
JANUARY DECEMBER 1996 & 1999

TABLE 12

Q14c. Type of Accommodation* (%)	Survey Year 1996						Survey Year 1999					
	US to Overseas	Leisure Env-Eco	Leisure Nati Prk	Lei/NP Env-Eco	Lei/NP Env/Camp	Business Env-Eco	US to Overseas	Leisure Env-Eco	Leisure Nati Prk	Lei/NP Env-Eco	Lei/NP Env/Camp	Business Env-Eco
(Number of Respondents)	27.343	789	1,645	395	159	230	27,221	818	1.749	411	159	172
Hotel / Hotel	71.5	76.4	67.5	78.3	68.2	85.6	70.0	81.3	69.7	88.4	89.0	82.8
Mean Nights in Dest.	8.3	10.2	11.0	12.3	11.6	14.6	8.2	10.4	10.9	10.5	12.2	11.6
Median Nights in Dest.	6.0	7.0	8.0	8.0	10.0	9.0	6.0	7.0	8.0	9.0	10.0	8.0
Private Home	35.6	28.9	43.7	30.5	40.3	35.6	36.7	25.4	43.0	24.4	25.0	27.5
Mean Nights in Dest.	17.0	17.7	18.9	20.2	23.2	22.2	15.7	12.2	18.8	14.1	16.9	54.9
Median Nights in Dest.	10.0	13.0	14.0	13.0	15.0	9.0	10.0	10.0	13.0	10.0	10.0	8.0
Other	6.1	13.7	12.2	15.2	20.2	9.6	5.4	10.3	8.8	10.6	10.2	8.9
Mean Nights in Dest.	18.3	9.0	11.0	6.9	6.1	46.5	13.6	8.8	13.1	11.8	11.4	16.5
Median Nights in Dest.	7.0	7.0	7.0	7.0	6.0	11.0	7.0	6.0	9.0	12.0	9.0	12.0

* Multiple Response.

TABLE 12a

Q14c. Overall Nights in Destination*	Survey Year 1996						Survey Year 1999					
	US to Overseas	Leisure Env-Eco	Leisure Nati Prk	Lei/NP Env-Eco	Lei/NP Env/Camp	Business Env-Eco	US to Overseas	Leisure Env-Eco	Leisure Nati Prk	Lei/NP Env-Eco	Lei/NP Env/Camp	Business Env-Eco
(Number of Respondents)	29,380	850	1.785	427	171	243	29,525	881	1,902	451	172	188
Mean Nights in Dest.	13.3	14.5	17.3	17.4	18.8	25.3	12.4	13.4	17.7	15.5	19.7	25.5
Median Nights in Dest.	8.0	10.0	14.0	13.0	14.0	11.0	8.0	9.0	13.0	12.0	15.0	10.0

* Multiple Response.

YEAR - TO - DATE

Cross Tab 1
Section 3

US TRAVELERS TO OVERSEAS AND MEXICO
PRODUCED FOR ECO TOURISM INTERNATIONAL
JANUARY DECEMBER 1996 & 1999

TABLE 13 Q13b. Nights Outside the U.S. (%)	Survey Year 1996						Survey Year 1999					
	US to Overseas	Leisure Env-Eco	Leisure Nati Prk	Lei/NP Env-Eco	Lei/NP Env/Camp	Business Env-Eco	US to Overseas	Leisure Env-Eco	Leisure Nati Prk	Lei/NP Env-Eco	Lei/NP Env/Camp	Business Env-Eco
(Number of Respondents)	34.796	1,015	2,133	510	205	258	35.190	1,007	2,280	508	194	206
Day Trip	–	–	–	–	–	–	–	–	–	–	–	–
1 - 3 Nights	12.0	3.5	3.4	3.5	5.7	3.5	10.4	6.8	3.2	1.8	1.1	2.6
4 - 7 Nights	30.5	27.4	16.0	16.4	13.0	20.4	32.6	25.4	14.2	15.1	7.2	32.6
8 - 10 Nights	14.6	16.6	12.9	15.3	14.4	17.2	16.2	14.3	13.5	13.9	10.0	12.2
11 - 14 Nights	14.7	17.8	19.1	18.4	17.8	19.1	15.3	16.9	17.9	16.2	11.5	12.9
15 - 21 Nights	13.8	17.2	22.6	22.1	20.4	12.3	13.7	20.8	24.8	30.9	42.6	9.7
22 - 28 Nights	3.9	3.6	8.3	4.7	6.7	4.1	3.2	4.7	7.0	7.8	7.5	5.9
29 - 35 Nights	4.8	7.6	10.0	11.5	10.5	6.1	4.2	3.7	11.3	5.8	7.0	9.0
36 or more Nights	5.7	6.3	7.8	8.3	11.5	17.3	4.5	7.3	8.2	8.5	13.2	15.2
Mean No. Nights	15.4	16.2	19.3	19.7	21.6	26.4	13.9	16.7	21.1	20.2	25.3	26.4
Median No. Nights	9.0	12.0	14.0	14.0	14.0	12.0	9.0	12.0	15.0	16.0	18.0	12.0

YEAR - TO - DATE

US TRAVELERS TO OVERSEAS AND MEXICO
PRODUCED FOR ECO TOURISM INTERNATIONAL
JANUARY DECEMBER 1996 & 1999

Cross Tab 1
Section 3

TABLE 14
Q27a. First Intl U.S. Trip (%)

	Survey Year 1996						Survey Year 1999					
	US to Overseas	Leisure Env-Eco	Leisure Nati Prk	Lei/NP Env-Eco	Lei/NP Env/Camp	Business Env-Eco	US to Overseas	Leisure Env-Eco	Leisure Nati Prk	Lei/NP Env-Eco	Lei/NP Env/Camp	Business Env-Eco
(Number of Respondents)	29.940	885	1.875	451	187	240	29.669	868	2.020	456	176	188
Yes	7.1	4.7	8.1	5.6	1.9	2.5	6.2	6.1	7.5	5.3	5.6	0.5
No	92.9	95.3	91.9	94.4	98.1	97.5	93.8	93.9	92.5	94.7	94.4	99.5

YEAR - TO - DATE

US TRAVELERS TO OVERSEAS AND MEXICO
PRODUCED FOR ECO TOURISM INTERNATIONAL
JANUARY DECEMBER 1996 & 1999

Cross Tab 1
Section 3

TABLE 15
Q27b. Int'l Trips Last 12 Months (%)

	Survey Year 1996						Survey Year 1999					
	US to Overseas	Leisure Env-Eco	Leisure Nati Prk	Lei/NP Env-Eco	Lei/NP Env/Camp	Business Env-Eco	US to Overseas	Leisure Env-Eco	Leisure Nati Prk	Lei/NP Env-Eco	Lei/NP Env/Camp	Business Env-Eco
(Number of Respondents)	29.949	885	1.875	451	187	240	29.678	868	2.020	456	176	188
1 Trip	42.4	51.1	51.3	49.9	43.8	23.1	42.4	56.4	56.9	53.0	53.1	33.5
2 or 3 Trips	32.0	35.6	35.1	34.9	41.5	30.7	32.1	30.2	30.8	32.8	33.3	28.5
4 or 5 Trips	10.5	8.3	8.3	7.9	9.2	16.5	11.1	6.8	6.6	7.9	2.3	13.4
6 or 10 Trips	10.4	4.8	5.1	7.2	5.5	20.7	10.2	5.9	5.6	6.3	11.3	20.1
11 or more Trips	4.8	0.2	0.2	0.2	–	9.1	4.1	0.8	0.2	–	–	4.5
Mean No. Trips	3.3	2.1	2.1	2.2	2.3	4.7	3.2	2.1	2.0	2.1	2.2	3.7
Median No. Trips	2.0	1.0	1.0	2.0	2.0	3.0	2.0	1.0	1.0	1.0	1.0	2.0

YEAR - TO - DATE

Cross Tab 1
Section 3

US TRAVELERS TO OVERSEAS AND MEXICO
PRODUCED FOR ECO TOURISM INTERNATIONAL
JANUARY DECEMBER 1996 & 1999

TABLE 16

Q27c. Int'l Trips Last 5 Years (%)	Survey Year 1996						Survey Year 1999					
	US to Overseas	Leisure Env-Eco	Leisure Nati Prk	Lei/NP Env-Eco	Lei/NP Env/Camp	Business Env-Eco	US to Overseas	Leisure Env-Eco	Leisure Nati Prk	Lei/NP Env-Eco	Lei/NP Env/Camp	Business Env-Eco
(Number of Respondents)	29.906	885	1.875	451	187	240	29,638	868	2.020	456	176	187
1 Trip	12.3	13.7	15.3	15.5	10.8	4.8	11.8	16.1	14.9	15.4	18.1	3.1
2 or 3 Trips	19.7	20.5	22.1	20.9	24.0	7.3	19.9	22.1	25.3	22.1	24.3	23.8
4 or 5 trips	16.0	17.2	18.0	15.9	13.3	13.4	16.3	20.9	21.1	18.7	18.6	9.6
6 - 10 Trips	21.0	29.0	24.7	24.2	31.0	19.1	22.2	22.4	22.4	24.2	21.4	22.4
11 - 15 Trips	9.4	8.3	7.4	8.6	6.4	13.6	9.1	8.2	7.3	6.9	2.8	15.5
16 or more Trips	21.6	11.4	12.5	15.0	14.4	41.8	20.8	10.4	9.0	12.7	15.0	25.6
Mean No. Trips	12.3	8.1	8.0	9.3	9.0	19.9	11.9	7.3	7.2	7.6	7.6	15.0
Median No. Trips	6.0	5.0	5.0	5.0	6.0	12.0	6.0	5.0	4.0	s.0	4.0	9.0

YEAR - TO - DATE

US TRAVELERS TO OVERSEAS AND MEXICO PRODUCED FOR ECO TOURISM INTERNATIONAL JANUARY DECEMBER 1996 & 1999

TABLE 17

Q14b. Number of Countries Visited* (%)	Survey Year 1996						Survey Year 1999					
	US to Overseas	Leisure Env-Eco	Leisure Nati Prk	Lei/NP Env-Eco	Lei/NP Env/Camp	Business Env-Eco	US to Overseas	Leisure Env-Eco	Leisure Nati Prk	Lei/NP Env-Eco	Lei/NP Env/Camp	Business Env-Eco
(Number of Respondents)	36,686	1.045	2.220	530	215	261	37.079	1.032	2.356	519	198	213
1 Country	80.3	81.2	74.6	77.1	77.8	60.4	81.3	77.7	73.3	67.4	64.5	80.5
2 Countries	12.1	12.8	16.4	14.2	13.6	18.0	11.9	14.0	17.8	21.1	22.8	14.6
3 Countries	4.4	3.3	4.5	4.7	3.5	12.3	3.9	7.1	5.9	9.8	8.8	4.6
4 Countries	1.6	0.9	1.8	1.4	0.3	2.4	1.5	0.3	1.7	0.5	0.9	0.3
5 or more Countries	1.5	1.7	2.7	2.6	4.8	6.9	1.4	1.0	1.3	1.3	2.9	–
Mean No. Countries	1.3	1.3	1.4	1.4	1.5	1.8	1.3	1.3	1.4	1.5	1.6	1.2
Median No. Countries	1.0	1.0	1.0	1.0	1.0	1.0	1.0	1.0	1.0	1.0	1.0	1.0
Median No. Trips	6.0	5.0	5.0	5.0	6.0	12.0	6.0	s.0	4.0	s.0	4.0	9.0

*Maximum Number Listed is Seven

YEAR - TO - DATE

Cross Tab 1
Section 3

US TRAVELERS TO OVERSEAS AND MEXICO
PRODUCED FOR ECO TOURISM INTERNATIONAL
JANUARY DECEMBER 1996 & 1999

TABLE 18

Q14d. Number of Destinations Listed* (%)	Survey Year 1996						Survey Year 1999					
	US to Overseas	Leisure Env-Eco	Leisure Nati Prk	Lei/NP Env-Eco	Lei/NP Env/Camp	Business Env-Eco	US to Overseas	Leisure Env-Eco	Leisure Nati Prk	Lei/NP Env-Eco	Lei/NP Env/Camp	Business Env-Eco
(Number of Respondents)	36,686	1.045	2,220	530	215	261	37.079	1.032	2.356	519	198	213
1 Destination	59.2	47.3	42.9	37.9	40.0	43.6	60.5	43.3	43.3	27.8	16.9	53.4
2 Destinations	20.6	20.8	23.5	24.1	25.7	19.5	21.0	25.2	21.3	23.7	31.7	24.6
3 Destinations	9.8	13.8	12.2	13.3	12.9	11.3	8.6	12.4	14.8	20.5	23.5	12.2
4 Destinations	4.8	9.6	8.7	11.7	3.2	11.5	4.5	7.7	7.1	10.5	11.8	5.7
5 Destinations	2.6	4.6	6.0	7.6	9.9	6.0	2.5	5.0	6.0	8.7	4.0	3.0
6 Destinations	1.5	1.8	2.7	2.4	2.9	4.7	1.5	3.4	4.2	3.8	5.5	1.1
7 Destinations	1.7	2.0	4.1	3.1	5.4	3.4	1.4	3.0	3.3	5.0	6.5	–
Mean No. Dest.	1.0	2.0	2.0	2.0	2.0	2.0	1.0	2.0	2.0	2.0	3.0	1.0
Median No. Dest.	1.0	2.0	2.0	2.0	2.0	2.0	1.0	2.0	2.0	2.0	3.0	1.0

*Maximum Number Listed is Seven

YEAR - TO - DATE

Cross Tab 1
Section 3

US TRAVELERS TO OVERSEAS AND MEXICO
PRODUCED FOR ECO TOURISM INTERNATIONAL
JANUARY DECEMBER 1996 & 1999

TABLE 19

Q18. Transportation Outside U.S.* (%)	Survey Year 1996						Survey Year 1999					
	US to Overseas	Leisure Env-Eco	Leisure Nati Prk	Lei/NP Env-Eco	Lei/NP Env/Camp	Business Env-Eco	US to Overseas	Leisure Env-Eco	Leisure Nati Prk	Lei/NP Env-Eco	Lei/NP Env/Camp	Business Env-Eco
(Number of Respondents)	33,411	998	2,144	512	206	255	33,411	992	2,278	509	195	205
Airline between Cities	34.2	46.5	43.8	49.9	53.2	49.6	34.2	53.4	48.2	62.0	74.5	56.5
Bus between Cities	14.6	24.1	27.4	31.0	26.8	16.1	13.1	21.9	23.4	26.6	25.2	11.0
City Subway / Tram / Bus	18.5	23.6	26.9	26.9	27.9	20.9	19.3	20.3	27.5	25.1	25.9	33.0
Company or Private Auto	28.7	23.9	28.3	23.4	25.9	42.7	27.9	23.9	30.8	23.9	28.4	37.6
Railroad between Cities	14.8	16.3	17.3	18.4	19.7	18.3	16.6	14.5	19.3	17.9	17.9	17.9
Rented Auto	19.5	27.5	26.5	31.7	35.8	20.1	19.7	23.5	27.1	29.7	36.5	26.8
Motor Home / Camper	1.5	2.4	3.1	2.6	2.8	2.2	0.4	1.5	1.2	1.6	3.1	–
Taxi / Cab / Limousine	48.4	41.8	39.3	43.2	44.0	53.9	47.9	50.1	41.6	47.3	49.0	51.3

*Multiple Response.

YEAR - TO - DATE

US TRAVELERS TO OVERSEAS AND MEXICO
PRODUCED FOR ECO TOURISM INTERNATIONAL
JANUARY DECEMBER 1996 & 1999

TABLE 20

Q4. Port of Entry (%)	Survey Year 1996						Survey Year 1999					
	US to Overseas	Leisure Env-Eco	Leisure Nati Prk	Lei/NP Env-Eco	Lei/NP Env/Camp	Business Env-Eco	US to Overseas	Leisure Env-Eco	Leisure Nati Prk	Lei/NP Env-Eco	Lei/NP Env/Camp	Business Env-Eco
(Number of Respondents)	36,686	1,045	2,220	530	215	261	37,079	1,032	2,356	519	198	213
Atlanta, GA	3.8	2.4	1.6	2.0	3.5	2.0	3.2	1.1	1.5	1.9	2.1	0.8
Baltimore, MD	1.2	1.6	1.6	0.8	0.1	0.2	0.2	0.5	0.4	0.4	0.6	0.3
Boston. MA	2.8	1.4	1.5	0.4	–	2.5	5.0	3.8	3.9	5.1	0.2	2.5
Charlotte, NC	1.7	5.0	1.7	3.8	0.7	0.2	2.0	3.8	1.1	1.1	0.7	0.1
Chicago. IL	4.8	3.3	3.9	3.5	1.8	5.2	6.8	2.7	5.4	3.6	4.3	5.0
Cincinnati, OH	0.6	0.4	0.4	0.1	0.1	–	0.9	0.2	0.4	0.2	–	2.3
Dallas / Ft. Worth, TX	3.4	3.0	1.8	2.3	4.5	0.7	5.7	3.3	4.0	2.0	0.8	1.0
Detroit, MI	1.3	0.5	0.6	0.6	–	1.2	1.2	0.2	0.7	–	–	0.4
Honolulu, HI	0.9	1.9	2.4	3.6	5.4	2.3	1.0	0.9	1.9	1.4	2.6	5.4
Houston. TX	2.6	3.7	2.5	2.3	2.5	3.9	4.3	10.0	5.8	10.3	8.9	8.8
Los Angeles. CA	12.3	12.6	17.6	15.3	21.7	14.1	9.6	14.2	19.3	24.0	28.4	11.7
Miami. FL	10.8	21.1	14.4	28.3	15.5	25.7	7.5	11.9	6.9	9.9	7.9	10.7
Minn. / St. Paul. MN	0.5	0.2	0.5	–	–	0.7	0.5	0.2	0.6	0.5	–	0.4
New York. NY	20.3	15.8	16.6	13.0	16.2	12.3	17.5	15.3	13.7	13.0	16.3	10.0
Newark. NJ	2.1	0.4	1.7	0.2	0.4	1.7	5.6	3.9	5.1	1.9	1.2	7.1
Orlando. FL	0.2	0.8	0.5	0.6	–	–	0.1	0.2	–	–	–	–
Philadelphia, PA	2.8	1.1	1.3	1.4	2.2	0.3	1.6	3.3	1.8	4.4	5.4	0.5
San Francisco	6.6	6.7	8.7	8.4	7.7	10.8	8.3	7.6	11.6	10.3	12.7	11.3
Seattle, WA	1.7	0.9	1.9	1.3	0.7	0.6	1.6	0.7	2.1	1.3	2.1	3.6
Washington. DC	4.6	2.7	4.3	3.9	6.8	8.4	3.1	2.3	3.4	2.1	2.0	8.3
Other Port	14.8	14.6	13.3	8.2	10.1	7.2	14.2	13.8	10.5	6.5	4.0	9.9

YEAR - TO - DATE

**Cross Tab 1
Section 3**

US TRAVELERS TO OVERSEAS AND MEXICO PRODUCED FOR ECO TOURISM INTERNATIONAL JANUARY DECEMBER 1996 & 1999

TABLE 21

Q2b. Main Destination (%)	Survey Year 1996						Survey Year 1999					
(Number of Respondents)	US to Overseas	Leisure Env-Eco	Leisure Nati Prk	Lei/NP Env-Eco	Lei/NP Env/Camp	Business Env-Eco	US to Overseas	Leisure Env-Eco	Leisure Nati Prk	Lei/NP Env-Eco	Lei/NP Env/Camp	Business Env-Eco
	34.825	985	2.064	494	196	241	35.273	966	2.189	474	184	201
EUROPE	32.9	15.8	23.6	13.7	16.0	17.8	36.0	16.7	25.3	16.5	11.7	19.2
WESTERN EUROPE	30.3	15.1	22.3	13.1	16.0	34.3	16.2	24.4	16.2	11.3	19.0	–
Austria	0.4	0.2	0.1	–	–	–	0.4	0.1	–	0.1	–	–
Belgium	0.5	0.4	0.2	–	–	0.7	0.6	–	–	–	–	–
Denmark	0.4	1.2	1.0	1.7	–	–	0.2	–	0.1	–	–	0.4
Finland	0.1	–	–	–	–	–	0.1	0.2	0.2	0.5	0.5	–
France	4.3	2.3	2.0	1.1	1.3	1.3	5.4	1.3	2.7	1.1	1.3	1.8
Germany	4.4	1.3	2.2	1.4	1.9	3.0	4.6	2.0	3.1	1.7	–	2.0
Greece	1.2	1.4	1.1	0.8	–	1.4	0.9	1.1	1.0	0.3	0.4	–
Iceland	–	–	–	–	–	–	0.1	0.5	0.2	0.4	0.3	0.7
Ireland	0.8	1.9	1.7	2.2	5.6	–	0.6	0.2	0.3	–	–	–
Italy	3.8	1.4	1.4	1.2	1.2	1.2	4.4	1.9	2.8	1.2	2.2	1.6
Luxembourg	–	–	–	–	–	0.3	–	–	–	–	–	–
Netherlands	1.5	0.2	0.4	0.2	–	1.4	1.8	0.6	1.1	0.7	0.4	1.3
Norway	0.4	0.1	0.1	0.1	–	–	0.2	0.1	0.2	0.2	0.4	1.0
Portugal	0.1	–	–	–	–	0.1	0.3	0.1	0.1	0.2	0.4	–
Spain	1.7	0.6	1.6	0.6	1.1	1.3	2.2	1.8	2.8	2.2	0.5	1.4
Sweden	0.4	0.2	0.2	0.3	0.1	0.2	0.5	0.3	0.4	0.5	–	0.2
Switzerland	1.3	1.0	0.3	–	0.1	1.5	1.1	1.5	0.6	1.0	1.1	0.4
United Kingdon	8.2	1.8	8.8	2.1	0.7	3.3	10.4	3.9	8.4	5.3	1.9	8.2
Other Western Europe	0.5	1.1	1.3	1.2	3.1	0.2	0.5	0.4	0.3	0.8	1.8	–

Continued....

YEAR - TO - DATE

**Cross Tab 1
Section 3**

US TRAVELERS TO OVERSEAS AND MEXICO
PRODUCED FOR ECO TOURISM INTERNATIONAL
JANUARY DECEMBER 1996 & 1999

TABLE 21

Q2b. Main Destination (%)	Survey Year 1996						Survey Year 1999					
	US to Overseas	Leisure Env-Eco	Leisure Nati Prk	Lei/NP Env-Eco	Lei/NP Env/Camp	Business Env-Eco	US to Overseas	Leisure Env-Eco	Leisure Nati Prk	Lei/NP Env-Eco	Lei/NP Env/Camp	Business Env-Eco
EASTERN EUROPE	2.6	0.7	1.3	0.5	0.8	1.8	1.7	0.5	0.9	0.3	0.5	0.2
Czech Republic	0.2	–	0.1	–	–	0.1	0.2	–	–	–	–	–
Hungary	0.3	0.2	0.3	0.1	0.3	–	0.2	–	0.3	–	–	–
Poland	0.6	0.4	0.6	0.3	0.3	0.1	0.6	0.4	0.5	0.2	0.2	0.1
Roniania	0.1	–	0.2	–	–	–	0.1	0.1	0.1	0.1	0.2	–
Russia	1.0	–	0.1	–	0.1	0.3	0.2	–	–	–	–	–
Ukraine	0.1	–	–	–	–	1.0	0.1	–	–	–	–	–
Other Estern Europe	0.3	0.1	0.1	–	0.1	0.4	0.2	–	–	–	–	0.1
CARIBBEAN	16.5	16.5	21.1	11.3	11.4	9.8	14.5	12.4	6.6	6.4	6.9	5.2
Antigua & Barbura	0.3	0.2	–	–	–	–	0.1	–	–	–	–	–
Aruba	0.2	–	–	–	–	–	0.2	0.3	0.2	0.8	1.8	–
Bahamas	6.5	3.8	2.2	0.9	0.7	–	4.3	2.3	1.0	0.3	0.7	–
Barbados	0.8	0.5	1.2	0.1	–	–	0.3	0.5	–	–	–	–
Bermuda	1.2	1.7	1.5	1.7	2.4	0.5	1.3	1.7	0.7	1.6	0.2	3.9
Cayman Is.	0.2	0.4	0.4	0.8	–	–	0.7	0.7	0.5	0.3	0.1	–
Dominican Rep	1.0	0.8	0.4	1.7	–	–	1.1	–	–	–	–	–
Haiti	0.2	–	–	–	–	–	0.3	–	0.1	–	–	1.1
Jamaica	4.3	5.1	4.5	3.0	7.7	0.1	5.1	5.1	3.1	3.2	4.1	–
Other Neth. Antilles	0.2	0.6	0.3	0.4	0.8	–	0.3	0.1	0.1	0.2	–	–
Trinidad&Tobago	1.2	2.2	0.6	0.9	–	9.2	0.5	0.2	0.7	–	–	0.1
Other Caribbean	0.5	1.3	0.9	1.8	–	–	0.4	1.6	0.3	–	–	–

YEAR - TO - DATE

Cross Tab 1
Section 3

US TRAVELERS TO OVERSEAS AND MEXICO PRODUCED FOR ECO TOURISM INTERNATIONAL JANUARY DECEMBER 1996 & 1999

TABLE 21

Q2b. Main Destination (%)	Survey Year 1996						Survey Year 1999					
	US to Overseas	Leisure Env-Eco	Leisure Nati Prk	Lei/NP Env-Eco	Lei/NP Env/Camp	Business Env-Eco	US to Overseas	Leisure Env-Eco	Leisure Nati Prk	Lei/NP Env-Eco	Lei/NP Env/Camp	Business Env-Eco
SOUTH AMERICA	6.7	11.8	8.0	11.1	10.1	11.3	6.5	12.4	7.2	10.5	12.0	16.2
Argentina	0.6	0.1	0.4	0.1	–	–	0.8	1.2	1.1	1.9	1.2	4.6
Brazil	1.4	1.7	1.0	0.9	2.1	0.6	1.6	1.5	1.5	1.5	1.1	6.2
Chile	0.5	0.6	0.8	1.3	2.5	3.3	0.4	1.5	0.4	0.3	0.5	–
Colombia	0.9	–	0.3	–	–	3.1	1.0	0.5	0.6	–	–	–
Ecuador	0.4	2.3	1.0	1.7	1.3	1.9	0.7	1.5	0.5	0.7	–	–
Peru	1.2	5.4	2.1	5.0	0.4	2.4	1.1	3.9	1.7	2.3	2.0	1.0
Venezuela	1.3	1.4	2.0	1.5	2.8	–	0.8	2.1	1.2	3.4	7.1	3.0
Other South America	0.5	0.4	0.2	0.7	0.9	–	0.2	0.1	0.4	0.3	–	1.3
CENTRAL AMERICA	22.1	36.1	24.3	35.7	29.7	17.6	21.7	30.9	20.2	21.1	11.8	15.6
Belize	0.2	1.6	0.4	1.0	0.8	1.2	0.1	0.8	0.4	1.7	3.3	–
Costa Rica	0.8	10.4	6.9	18.7	11.5	2.0	1.0	4.0	3.9	6.4	5.5	–
El Salvador	0.2	–	0.2	–	–	–	0.3	–	–	–	–	–
Guatemala	0.6	0.6	0.6	1.1	1.0	2.4	0.4	0.1	–	–	–	–
Honduras	0.4	0.4	0.2	0.4	0.9	–	0.1	–	–	–	–	–
Panama	0.4	0.6	1.2	0.6	–	0.7	0.3	0.1	0.2	0.3	0.6	2.3
Other Central America	19.3	22.4	14.8	13.9	15.5	11.4	19.4	25.8	15.7	12.7	2.3	13.3
AFRICA	1.6	4.9	5.6	7.8	7.1	6.5	1.4	5.2	5.4	7.9	9.3	10.3
Kenya	0.2	1.8	1.8	3.1	4.6	0.4	0.2	1.8	2.3	4.2	8.4	6.4
Morocco	0.2	0.1	0.1	0.1	0.1	–	0.3	0.4	0.2	0.3	0.1	–
South Africa	0.5	2.1	1.9	3.2	0.7	3.0	0.4	1.7	2.1	2.7	0.6	0.8
Zimbabwe	–	0.2	0.4	0.4	0.9	–	–	–	0.5	0.1	0.1	0.3
Other Africa	0.6	0.8	1.5	1.0	0.8	3.1	0.2	1.2	0.3	0.7	–	2.8

Continued...

YEAR - TO - DATE

**Cross Tab 1
Section 3**

US TRAVELERS TO OVERSEAS AND MEXICO PRODUCED FOR ECO TOURISM INTERNATIONAL JANUARY DECEMBER 1996 & 1999

TABLE 21

Q2b. Main Destination (%)	Survey Year 1996						Survey Year 1999					
	US to Overseas	Leisure Env-Eco	Leisure Nati Prk	Lei/NP Env-Eco	Lei/NP Env/Camp	Business Env-Eco	US to Overseas	Leisure Env-Eco	Leisure Nati Prk	Lei/NP Env-Eco	Lei/NP Env/Camp	Business Env-Eco
MIDDLE EAST	3.7	2.4	2.9	1.4	0.3	9.3	3.0	2.7	3.5	4.0	2.9	2.0
Egypt	0.3	0.4	0.7	0.2	–	0.5	0.2	0.1	–	–	–	–
Israel	0.9	0.6	0.4	0.3	–	1.4	1.0	0.7	0.7	0.6	1.1	0.1
Jordan	0.1	–	0.1	–	–	–	–	–	–	–	–	–
Kuwait	0.1	–	–	–	–	–	0.1	–	–	–	–	–
Saudi Arabia	0.4	0.1	0.2	0.2	–	0.4	0.1	–	0.1	–	–	0.7
Turkey	1.4	1.1	1.3	0.7	0.3	5.9	0.8	1.9	1.4	3.3	1.6	–
United Arab Emirates	0.1	–	–	–	–	0.7	0.4	–	0.9	–	–	1.2
Other Middle East	0.4	0.2	0.1	–	–	0.4	0.4	–	0.3	0.1	0.2	–
ASIA	14.2	5.3	13.1	8.0	8.2	19.7	14.2	9.6	18.2	15.6	23.7	15.5
Hong Kong	1.7	0.3	1.1	0.5	–	0.2	1.5	0.3	1.3	0.2	0.1	2.5
India	1.0	0.3	0.9	0.3	0.1	0.6	1.3	2.3	1.7	3.9	8.2	0.9
Indonesia	0.4	0.3	0.5	0.4	0.4	0.6	0.2	0.7	0.6	1.3	1.9	1.0
Japan	2.8	0.8	1.7	1.1	2.2	4.6	3.4	0.6	2.7	1.0	1.6	2.1
Korea. South	1.9	0.7	2.3	1.6	2.6	–	1.9	0.6	2.6	1.1	2.6	0.8
Malaysia	0.3	0.2	0.3	0.2	0.4	1.0	0.2	0.2	0.2	0.3	0.6	0.3
P. R. of China	1.0	0.4	0.3	0.6	0.1	2.7	1.3	0.9	1.5	1.3	2.2	1.7
Philippines	1.7	0.6	1.6	0.9	1.0	1.8	1.0	0.1	1.7	0.3	0.1	0.3
R. of China (Taiwan)	1.5	0.6	1.7	1.1	0.1	2.5	1.4	0.9	2.0	1.2	0.7	2.2
Singapore	0.6	0.3	0.3	0.5	0.4	0.4	0.6	0.3	0.2	0.5	–	2.1
Thailand	0.6	0.6	0.7	0.7	0.9	1.3	0.6	1.3	2.1	2.5	2.1	1.4
Vietnam	0.2	0.1	0.1	–	–	0.2	0.2	0.1	0.3	0.1	–	0.1
Other Asia	0.5	0.1	1.1	0.1	–	3.9	0.5	1.4	1.4	1.8	3.7	0.1
OCENIA	2.4	7.2	10.3	11.1	17.1	7.9	2.6	10.0	13.6	18.1	21.8	16.0
Australia	1.8	5.1	7.6	8.3	11.7	3.7	1.6	5.4	7.7	10.0	13.2	12.8
New Zealand	0.4	1.6	1.9	2.3	5.4	2.9	0.8	3.9	5.1	7.5	8.5	2.6
Other Oceania	0.2	0.5	0.8	0.5	–	1.4	0.2	0.8	0.8	0.6	0.1	0.6

YEAR - TO - DATE

US TRAVELERS TO OVERSEAS AND MEXICO
PRODUCED FOR ECO TOURISM INTERNATIONAL
JANUARY DECEMBER 1996 & 1999

TABLE 21

Q2b. Main Destination (%)

	Survey Year 1996						Survey Year 1999					
	US to Overseas	Leisure Env-Eco	Leisure Nati Prk	Lei/NP Env-Eco	Lei/NP Env/Camp	Business Env-Eco	US to Overseas	Leisure Env-Eco	Leisure Nati Prk	Lei/NP Env-Eco	Lei/NP Env/Camp	Business Env-Eco
MIDDLE EAST	3.7	2.4	2.9	1.4	0.3	9.3	3.0	2.7	3.5	4.0	2.9	2.0
Egypt	0.3	0.4	0.7	0.2	-	0.5	0.2	0.1	-	-	-	-
Israel	0.9	0.6	0.4	0.3	-	1.4	1.0	0.7	0.7	0.6	1.1	0.1
Jordan	0.1	-	0.1	-	-	-	-	-	-	-	-	-
Kuwait	0.1	-	-	-	-	-	0.1	-	-	-	-	-
Saudi Arabia	0.4	0.1	0.2	0.2	-	0.4	0.1	-	0.1	-	-	0.7
Turkey	1.4	1.1	1.3	0.7	0.3	5.9	0.8	1.9	1.4	3.3	1.6	-
United Arab Emirates	0.1	-	-	-	-	0.7	0.4	-	0.9	-	-	1.2
Other Middle East	0.4	0.2	0.1	-	-	0.4	0.4	-	0.3	0.1	0.2	-
ASIA	14.2	5.3	13.1	8.0	8.2	19.7	14.2	9.6	18.2	15.6	23.7	15.5
Hong Kong	1.7	0.3	1.1	0.5	-	0.2	1.5	0.3	1.3	0.2	0.1	2.5
India	1.0	0.3	0.9	0.3	0.1	0.6	1.3	2.3	1.7	3.9	8.2	0.9
Indonesia	0.4	0.3	0.5	0.4	0.4	0.6	0.2	0.7	0.6	1.3	1.9	1.0
Japan	2.8	0.8	1.7	1.1	2.2	4.6	3.4	0.6	2.7	1.0	1.6	2.1
Korea. South	1.9	0.7	2.3	1.6	2.6	-	1.9	0.6	2.6	1.1	2.6	0.8
Malaysia	0.3	0.2	0.3	0.2	0.4	1.0	0.2	0.2	0.2	0.3	0.6	0.3
P. R. of China	1.0	0.4	0.8	0.6	0.1	2.7	1.3	0.9	1.5	1.3	2.2	1.7
Philippines	1.7	0.6	1.6	0.9	1.0	1.8	1.0	0.1	1.7	0.3	0.1	0.3
R. of China (Taiwan)	1.5	0.6	1.7	1.1	0.1	2.5	1.4	0.9	2.0	1.2	0.7	2.2
Singapore	0.6	0.3	0.3	0.5	0.4	0.4	0.6	0.3	0.2	0.5	-	2.1
Thailand	0.6	0.6	0.7	0.7	0.9	1.3	0.6	1.3	2.1	2.5	2.1	1.4
Vietnam	0.2	0.1	0.1	-	-	0.2	0.2	0.1	0.3	0.1	-	0.1
Other Asia	0.5	0.1	1.1	0.1	-	3.9	0.5	1.4	1.4	1.8	3.7	0.1
OCENIA	2.4	7.2	10.3	11.1	17.1	7.9	2.6	10.0	13.6	18.1	21.8	16.0
Australia	1.8	5.1	7.6	8.3	11.7	3.7	1.6	5.4	7.7	10.0	13.2	12.8
New Zealand	0.4	1.6	1.9	2.3	5.4	2.9	0.8	3.9	5.1	7.5	8.5	2.6
Other Oceania	0.2	0.5	0.8	0.5	-	1.4	0.2	0.8	0.8	0.6	0.1	0.6

YEAR - TO - DATE

Cross Tab 1
Section 3

US TRAVELERS TO OVERSEAS AND MEXICO
PRODUCED FOR ECO TOURISM INTERNATIONAL
JANUARY DECEMBER 1996 & 1999

TABLE 21 Q2b. Main Destination (%) (Number of Respondents)	Survey Year 1996						Survey Year 1999					
	US to Overseas	Leisure Env-Eco	Leisure Nati Prk	Lei/NP Env-Eco	Lei/NP Env/Camp	Business Env-Eco	US to Overseas	Leisure Env-Eco	Leisure Nati Prk	Lei/NP Env-Eco	Lei/NP Env/Camp	Business Env-Eco
	36.686	1.045	2.220	530	215	261	37,079	1,032	2,356	519	198	213
EUROPE	36.0	18.7	29.0	17.5	21.8	24.3	38.5	20.6	28.4	21.5	17.5	25.5
WESTERN EUROPE	34.1	18.2	27.9	17.1	21.4	23.1	37.3	20.1	27.6	21.2	17.1	25.4
Austria	1.7	1.0	1.6	0.4	0.7	1.9	1.5	0.5	1.1	0.9	0.4	0.5
Belgium	1.3	0.5	0.6	0.2	-	2.5	1.6	0.9	0.8	1.8	2.0	0.3
Denmark	0.9	1.4	1.4	1.8	0.3	0.1	0.7	0.2	0.4	0.5	-	1.2
Finland	0.3	0.2	0.2	-	-	-	0.3	0.3	0.3	0.4	0.5	-
France	7.7	3.8	5.8	3.6	5.5	4.4	9.1	3.8	5.8	3.9	6.2	4.7
Germany	6.8	2.4	4.3	2.2	2.8	7.5	6.5	2.9	4.3	3.6	3.3	3.5
Greece	1.6	1.9	1.3	0.9	0.4	2.0	1.3	1.8	2.0	1.6	1.4	0.1
Icel and	-	-	-	-	-	-	0.2	0.7	0.3	0.6	0.8	0.7
Ireland	1.5	2.5	3.7	3.4	8.4	0.3	1.5	2.2	2.1	3.0	-	-
Italy	5.7	2.8	4.0	3.1	4.4	1.9	6.3	3.4	4.2	1.6	2.5	2.7
Luxembourg	0.1	-	-	-	-	0.7	0.2	-	-	-	-	-
Netherlands	3.2	1.3	2.5	2.1	3.4	3.4	3.5	2.5	3.6	4.0	6.1	2.4
Norway	0.6	0.9	1.0	1.9	0.2	-	0.5	0.2	0.6	0.4	0.4	1.9
Portugal	0.5	0.8	0.6	1.5	2.9	0.1	0.5	0.4	0.4	0.8	0.4	0.1
Spain	2.5	1.7	2.6	2.2	4.0	2.0	3.1	2.5	3.3	3.1	3.7	1.4
Sweden	0.8	1.3	1.1	2.0	0.1	0.4	0.9	0.4	0.6	0.6	0.4	-
Switzerland	2.9	1.6	2.5	1.0	1.3	1.6	2.6	1.6	2.0	0.9	1.0	2.0
United Kingdom	11.8	4.8	14.5	6.2	9.5	5.0	13.7	8.4	12.0	9.6	7.7	10.2
Other Western Europe	0.5	0.5	0.3	0.2	-	0.2	0.7	0.6	0.9	0.7	1.6	-

Continued....

YEAR - TO - DATE

Cross Tab 1
Section 3

US TRAVELERS TO OVERSEAS AND MEXICO
PRODUCED FOR ECO TOURISM INTERNATIONAL
JANUARY DECEMBER 1996 & 1999

TABLE 22

Q14a. International Destinations* (%)	Survey Year 1996						Survey Year 1999					
	US to Overseas	Leisure Env-Eco	Leisure Nati Prk	Lei/NP Env-Eco	Lei/NP Env/Camp	Business Env-Eco	US to Overseas	Leisure Env-Eco	Leisure Nati Prk	Lei/NP Env-Eco	Lei/NP Env/Camp	Business Env-Eco
EASTERN EUROPE	3.4	1.5	2.2	1.2	0.8	1.7	2.5	0.7	1.8	0.5	0.9	1.1
Czech Republic	0.6	0.4	0.4	0.3	–	0.1	0.7	0.1	0.5	–	–	–
Hungary	0.6	0.4	0.3	0.1	0.3	0.1	0.5	0.1	0.7	0.2	0.4	0.5
Poland	0.8	0.7	0.7	0.5	0.3	0.1	0.7	0.4	0.7	0.2	0.2	0.1
Romania	0.2	–	0.4	–	–	–	0.2	0.1	0.3	0.2	0.2	–
Russia	1.2	0.2	0.6	0.3	0.2	0.3	0.4	–	0.1	–	–	0.5
Ukraine	0.1	0.2	–	–	–	0.9	0.1	–	–	–	–	–
Other Eastern Europe	0.5	0.2	0.3	0.1	0.4	0.3	0.2	–	0.1	–	–	0.1
CARIBBEAN	16.0	16.6	11.7	12.2	11.5	9.0	14.1	11.8	6.3	5.7	6.3	5.0
Antigua & Barbua	0.3	0.4	0.1	0.4	0.5	–	0.1	–	–	–	–	–
Aruba	0.2	0.4	–	–	–	–	0.3	0.3	0.3	0.7	1.7	–
Bahamas	6.2	3.7	2.1	0.9	0.6	–	4.2	2.2	0.9	0.3	0.7	–
Barbados	0.8	0.6	1.4	0.6	–	4.0	0.4	0.5	–	–	–	–
Bermuda	1.1	1.5	1.3	1.4	2.3	0.5	1.2	1.6	0.9	1.4	0.2	3.8
Caytnan Is.	0.2	0.4	0.3	0.7	–	–	0.7	0.7	0.4	0.3	0.1	–
Dominican Rep.	1.0	0.8	0.4	1.6	–	–	1.1	–	–	–	–	–
Haiti	0.1	–	–	–	–	–	0.3	–	0.1	–	–	1.1
Jamaica	4.2	5.0	4.3	2.9	7.4	–	4.9	4.8	2.9	2.9	3.8	–
Other Neth. Antilles	0.2	1.1	0.5	1.5	0.7	–	0.3	0.1	–	0.2	–	–
Trinidad & Tobago	0.6	1.5	1.0	2.0	–	–	0.4	1.5	0.3	–	–	–

YEAR - TO - DATE

Cross Tab 1
Section 3

US TRAVELERS TO OVERSEAS AND MEXICO
PRODUCED FOR ECO TOURISM INTERNATIONAL
JANUARY DECEMBER 1996 & 1999

TABLE 22

Q14a. International Destinations* (%)	Survey Year 1996						Survey Year 1999					
	US to Overseas	Leisure Env-Eco	Leisure Nati Prk	Lei/NP Env-Eco	Lei/NP Env/Camp	Business Env-Eco	US to Overseas	Leisure Env-Eco	Leisure Nati Prk	Lei/NP Env-Eco	Lei/NP Env/Camp	Business Env-Eco
SOUTH AMERICA	6.9	12.2	8.3	11.6	10.5	15.3	6.8	13.3	7.4	11.9	12.4	17.2
Argentina	1.0	0.2	0.8	0.3	0.4	0.8	0.9	1.7	1.6	2.6	1.1	4.7
Brazil	1.6	1.8	1.1	1.0	2.4	1.4	1.8	2.5	1.7	2.2	1.0	7.9
Chile	0.7	0.7	1.1	1.5	2.9	3.0	0.6	2.6	1.0	1.8	0.9	1.9
Colombia	1.0	–	0.3	–	–	3.7	1.1	0.6	0.6	0.5	1.1	–
Ecuador	0.5	2.8	1.3	2.0	2.1	2.1	0.8	1.8	0.7	1.5	0.6	–
Peru	1.3	6.0	2.6	5.9	1.5	2.1	1.1	4.2	1.8	3.2	3.0	1.0
Venezuela	1.3	1.4	2.0	1.7	3.0	–	0.9	1.6	1.2	3.2	6.6	2.9
Other South America	0.6	0.4	0.3	0.7	1.1	3.8	0.3	0.7	0.6	1.1	1.3	2.2
CENTRAL AMERICA	21.5	35.3	23.4	35.0	29.1	18.9	21.0	29.3	19.0	19.0	10.9	15.2
Belize	0.2	2.2	0.7	2.2	1.2	1.6	0.1	0.8	0.3	1.5	3.1	–
Costa Rica	1.0	10.9	6.8	19.1	11.2	3.0	1.1	3.8	3.8	5.8	5.1	–
El Salvador	0.3	–	0.2	–	–	0.6	0.4	–	–	–	–	–
Guatemala	0.7	0.8	0.7	1.3	1.7	2.8	0.4	0.1	–	–	–	–
Honduras	0.8	0.5	0.3	0.6	0.9	0.3	0.1	–	–	–	–	–
Panama	0.8	0.9	1.3	1.4	–	1.5	0.5	0.1	0.2	0.3	0.6	2.3
Other Central America	18.8	22.0	14.4	13.9	15.3	11.1	18.9	24.4	14.8	11.4	2.1	12.9
AFRICA	1.9	5.1	6.0	8.1	7.2	7.8	1.7	5.8	6.1	8.3	10.0	10.2
Kenya	0.3	2.3	2.1	3.6	5.7	0.4	0.3	2.4	2.5	4.1	8.1	6.2
Morocco	0.3	0.2	0.2	0.2	0.1	–	0.4	0.6	0.5	0.7	0.5	–
South Africa	0.7	2.3	2.4	3.5	0.9	4.8	0.5	2.4	2.9	3.0	1.4	2.0
Zimbabwe	0.1	1.4	1.4	1.7	1.6	–	0.1	0.5	1.2	0.9	0.6	0.4
Other Africa	0.9	2.2	2.6	3.2	2.4	3.8	0.7	3.4	2.5	5.7	6.9	3.0

Continued...

YEAR - TO - DATE

**US TRAVELERS TO OVERSEAS AND MEXICO
PRODUCED FOR ECO TOURISM INTERNATIONAL
JANUARY DECEMBER 1996 & 1999**

Cross Tab 1
Section 3

TABLE 22

Q14a. International Destinations* (%)	Survey Year 1996						Survey Year 1999					
	US to Overseas	Leisure Env-Eco	Leisure Nati Prk	Lei/NP Env-Eco	Lei/NP Env/Camp	Business Env-Eco	US to Overseas	Leisure Env-Eco	Leisure Nati Prk	Lei/NP Env-Eco	Lei/NP Env/Camp	Business Env-Eco
MIDDLE EAST	4.6	4.0	3.4	1.9	1.4	10.7	3.5	3.5	4.2	4.9	2.6	2.0
Egypt	0.6	0.7	1.0	0.5	-	1.2	0.4	0.9	0.3	1.0	-	-
Israel	1.3	1.0	1.1	0.4	0.2	1.6	1.1	0.7	0.7	0.5	1.0	0.1
Jordan	0.2	0.1	0.1	-	-	0.9	0.1	0.1	0.1	0.2	-	-
Kuwait	0.2	-	-	-	-	-	0.1	-	0.1	0.1	-	-
Saudi Arabi	0.4	0.1	0.2	0.2	-	0.4	0.2	-	0.1	-	-	0.7
Turkey	1.9	2.3	1.5	0.8	0.4	6.6	1.1	1.9	1.7	3.2	1.5	-
United Arab Emirates	0.2	-	-	-	-	0.6	0.5	-	0.9	-	-	1.2
Other Middle East	0.6	0.2	0.2	-	-	1.1	0.4	0.1	0.3	0.1	0.2	-
ASIA	14.9	6.0	13.9	9.4	9.0	25.6	15.0	9.7	18.5	15.1	22.9	16.2
Hong Kong	3.1	1.3	3.1	2.4	1.0	4.4	2.6	0.8	2.4	1.2	1.7	2.9
India	1.3	0.3	1.3	0.4	0.4	4.9	1.6	2.5	2.2	4.1	8.4	0.9
Indonesia	0.8	0.6	1.0	0.8	0.6	4.5	0.4	0.7	0.8	1.3	2.1	1.0
Japan	3.6	1.0	2.1	1.5	2.3	7.5	4.2	1.4	3.8	2.2	3.5	3.1
Korea, South	2.3	0.7	2.9	1.6	2.5	1.1	2.3	3.5	2.5	1.0	2.4	1.1
Malaysia	0.6	0.4	0.7	0.8	1.2	2.2	0.4	0.3	0.3	0.4	0.7	0.4
P. R. of China	1.7	0.7	1.4	0.9	0.4	5.5	1.9	1.3	2.1	1.8	2.9	3.0
Philippines	2.0	0.6	1.5	0.9	0.9	2.8	1.1	0.1	1.8	0.3	0.1	0.7
R. of China (Taiwan)	2.1	0.9	2.1	1.4	1.0	5.3	1.9	1.0	2.2	1.3	0.7	2.5
Singapore	1.6	0.6	0.8	1.2	1.0	4.8	1.4	1.2	1.0	1.1	1.2	3.1
Thailand	1.3	1.0	1.6	1.4	2.3	3.4	1.2	2.2	3.2	4.0	5.0	1.5
Vietnam	0.3	0.4	0.4	0.6	-	1.6	0.2	0.1	0.3	0.2	-	0.2
Other Asia	0.8	0.3	1.5	0.4	0.5	7.8	0.8	1.8	2.3	2.6	4.9	0.1
OCEANIA	2.6	7.3	10.5	11.2	16.9	7.7	2.9	11.3	14.8	19.6	25.2	15.7
Australia	2.2	6.2	9.1	10.0	14.2	5.1	1.9	7.3	9.9	12.6	16.5	13.3
New Zealand	0.8	2.6	3.9	3.9	6.5	3.5	1.2	6.4	7.9	11.6	14.0	2.6
Other Oceania	0.1	0.3	0.8	0.4	0.7	2.2	0.3	2.2	1.9	3.3	4.6	0.6

* Multiniple Response.

YEAR - TO - DATE

US TRAVELERS TO OVERSEAS AND MEXICO
PRODUCED FOR ECO TOURISM INTERNATIONAL
JANUARY DECEMBER 1996 & 1999

Cross Tab 1
Section 3

TABLE 22

Q14a. International Destinations* (%)	Survey Year 1996						Survey Year 1999					
	US to Overseas	Leisure Env-Eco	Leisure Nati Prk	Lei/NP Env-Eco	Lei/NP Env/Camp	Business Env-Eco	US to Overseas	Leisure Env-Eco	Leisure Nati Prk	Lei/NP Env-Eco	Lei/NP Env/Camp	Business Env-Eco
MIDDLE EAST	4.6	4.0	3.4	1.9	1.4	10.7	3.5	3.5	4.2	4.9	2.6	2.0
Egypt	0.6	0.7	1.0	0.5	–	1.2	0.4	0.9	0.3	1.0	–	–
Israel	1.3	1.0	1.1	0.4	0.2	1.6	1.1	0.7	0.7	0.5	1.0	0.1
Jordan	0.2	0.1	0.1	–	–	0.9	0.1	0.1	0.1	0.2	–	–
Kuwait	0.2	–	–	–	–	–	0.1	–	0.1	0.1	–	–
Saudi Arabi	0.4	0.1	0.2	0.2	–	0.4	0.2	–	0.1	–	–	0.7
Turkey	1.9	2.3	1.5	0.8	0.4	6.6	1.1	1.9	1.7	3.2	1.5	–
United Arab Emirates	0.2	–	–	–	–	0.6	0.5	–	0.9	–	–	1.2
Other Middle East	0.6	0.2	0.2	–	–	1.1	0.4	0.1	0.3	0.1	0.2	–
ASIA	14.9	6.0	13.9	9.4	9.0	25.6	15.0	9.7	18.5	15.1	22.9	16.2
Hong Kong	3.1	1.3	3.1	2.4	1.0	4.4	2.6	0.8	2.4	1.2	1.7	2.9
India	1.3	0.3	1.3	0.4	0.4	4.9	1.6	2.5	2.2	4.1	8.4	0.9
Indonesia	0.8	0.6	1.0	0.8	0.6	4.5	0.4	0.7	0.8	1.3	2.1	1.0
Japan	3.6	1.0	2.1	1.5	2.3	7.5	4.2	1.4	3.8	2.2	3.5	3.1
Korea, South	2.3	0.7	2.9	1.6	2.5	1.1	2.3	3.5	2.5	1.0	2.4	1.1
Malaysia	0.6	0.4	0.7	0.8	1.2	2.2	0.4	0.3	0.3	0.4	0.7	0.4
P. R. of China	1.7	0.7	1.4	0.9	0.4	5.5	1.9	1.3	2.1	1.8	2.9	3.0
Philippines	2.0	0.6	1.5	0.9	0.9	2.8	1.1	0.1	1.8	0.3	0.1	0.7
R. of China (Taiwan)	2.1	0.9	2.1	1.4	1.0	5.3	1.9	1.0	2.2	1.3	0.7	2.5
Singapore	1.6	0.6	0.8	1.2	1.0	4.8	1.4	1.2	1.0	1.1	1.2	3.1
Thailand	1.3	1.0	1.6	1.4	2.3	3.4	1.2	2.2	3.2	4.0	5.0	1.5
Vietnam	0.3	0.4	0.4	0.6	–	1.6	0.2	0.1	0.3	0.2	–	0.2
Other Asia	0.8	0.3	1.5	0.4	0.5	7.8	0.8	1.8	2.3	2.6	4.9	0.1
OCEANIA	2.6	7.3	10.5	11.2	16.9	7.7	2.9	11.3	14.8	19.6	25.2	15.7
Australia	2.2	6.2	9.1	10.0	14.2	5.1	1.9	7.3	9.9	12.6	16.5	13.3
New Zealand	0.8	2.6	3.9	3.9	6.5	3.5	1.2	6.4	7.9	11.6	14.0	2.6
Other Oceania	0.1	0.3	0.8	0.4	0.7	2.2	0.3	2.2	1.9	3.3	4.6	0.6

* Multiple Response.

YEAR - TO - DATE

**Cross Tab 1
Section 3**

US TRAVELERS TO OVERSEAS AND MEXICO
PRODUCED FOR ECO TOURISM INTERNATIONAL
JANUARY DECEMBER 1996 & 1999

TABLE 23

Q19. Leisure Activities* (%)

	Survey Year 1996						Survey Year 1999					
(Number of Respondents)	US to Overseas	Leisure Env-Eco	Leisure Nati Prk	Lei/NP Env-Eco	Lei/NP Env/Camp	Business Env-Eco	US to Overseas	Leisure Env-Eco	Leisure Nati Prk	Lei/NP Env-Eco	Lei/NP Env/Camp	Business Env-Eco
	32.318	1,045	2.220	530	215	261	32,4	32	2,356	519	198	213
Amusement / Theme Parks	10.2	14.9	26.4	21.2	27.1	10.1	9.9	12.4	22.9	16.2	12.6	17.8
Art Gallery / Museum	23.8	38.8	44.7	43.5	58.1	36.4	26.7	37.4	49.5	51.6	56.3	43.4
Attend Sports Event	3.9	10.5	12.7	16.1	29.3	3.7	3.9	7.5	9.0	7.3	11.0	11.8
Camping / Hiking	4.8	27.6	20.4	40.0	100.0	17.8	4.7	29.6	24.2	42.3	100.0	26.8
Casinos / Gambling	9.5	12.3	11.1	14.8	20.7	2.9	7.0	7.8	8.8	8.1	9.1	2.9
Concert / Play / Musical	12.9	22.2	28.6	30.9	47.7	15.4	13.8	19.8	29.4	28.0	31.9	34.7
Cruise. 1 Night +	5.6	19.6	11.4	22.2	28.3	5.2	4.4	13.7	7.4	12.8	9.7	7.2
Cultural Heritage Sites	30.1	60.9	60.9	73.3	82.4	46.6	29.3	63.2	59.0	79.2	87.7	47.6
Dining in Restaurants	84.4	78.1	84.5	82.8	92.5	76.5	85.2	85.4	89.1	95.6	95.0	82.0
Environ. / Eco. Excursions	4.8	100.0	25.1	100.0	100.0	100.0	4.2	100.0	22.7	100.0	100.0	100.0
Ethnic Heritage Sites	14.3	40.2	35.9	45.5	54.2	28.0	12.6	38.4	34.8	53.0	64.4	24.2
Golfing / Tennis	8.5	11.6	9.2	11.5	23.2	7.7	7.2	10.9	6.8	11.5	21.5	12.6
Guided Tours	16.1	32.7	29.9	33.8	39.1	13.7	16.4	38.0	32.0	46.5	41.7	13.4
Hunting / Fishing	4.1	9.9	9.5	12.0	16.9	3.8	4.2	13.3	8.8	13.2	18.5	3.3
Nightclubs / dancing	26.1	36.6	37.4	37.5	55.4	19.4	25.0	35.4	31.4	34.5	39.1	26.1
Ranch Vacations	2.3	6.9	7.8	12.1	21.0	2.9	1.8	6.5	5.8	9.3	10.7	0.5
Shopping	74.5	77.3	83.6	81.8	87.5	56.8	75.2	82.1	85.2	90.3	90.2	72.7
Sightseeing in Cities	40.3	58.5	67.5	65.8	77.5	37.2	43.0	60.3	69.8	75.6	78.0	46.1
Snow Skiing	1.9	3.8	2.4	5.7	13.2	5.7	1.5	2.2	2.6	1.5	2.9	7.3
Touring Countryside	36.7	73.4	74.8	84.9	93.9	53.9	34.9	69.0	71.3	84.0	90.7	47.1
Visit Historical Places	50.4	70.1	80.9	77.8	80.9	62.8	51.0	69.6	79.4	82.5	82.9	64.1
Visit National Parks	8.9	46.8	100.0	100.0	100.0	29.3	8.4	45.5	100.0	100.0	100.0	46.0
Visit Small Towns	42.4	74.7	75.7	83.1	89.1	51.	42.1	69.7	74.9	87.4	94.0	64.4
Water Sports / Sunbathing	28.8	57.8	44.0	58.4	71.5	27.6	26.0	56.1	41.6	55.8	68.6	36.6

*Multiple Response.

World Tourism Organization

YEAR - TO - DATE

US TRAVELERS TO OVERSEAS AND MEXICO
PRODUCED FOR ECO TOURISM INTERNATIONAL
JANUARY DECEMBER 1996 & 1999

TABLE 24

Q16. Total Trip expenditures

	Survey Year 1996						Survey Year 1999					
	US to Overseas	Leisure Env-Eco	Leisure Nati Prk	Lei/NP Env-Eco	Lei/NP Env/Camp	Business Env-Eco	US to Overseas	Leisure Env-Eco	Leisure Nati Prk	Lei/NP Env-Eco	Lei/NP Env/Camp	Business Env-Eco
Mean Total Trip Expenditure												
(Number of Respondents)	25,818	769	1.618	397	157	208	25,389	767	1.736	386	151	159
Per Travel Party / Trip	$4,149	$3,776	$4,213	$4,271	$4,624	$5,069	$3,898	$4,602	$4,801	$6,152	$8,420	$4,888
Per Visitor I Trip	$2,671	$2,105	$2,335	$2,396	$2,752	$3,930	$2,534	$2,435	$2,737	$3,279	$4,314	$3,570
Mean Package Price												
(Number of Respondents)	3,469	240	408	126	35	12	3,747	270	462	137	45	9
Per Travel party / Trip	$3,554	$4,271	$4,630	$4,638	$5,850	$5,933	$4,116	$5,669	$7,538	$8,172	$10,445	$3,682
Per Visitor / Trip	$1,621	$2,052	$2,079	$2,196	$2,668	$1,983	$1,871	$2,687	$3,601	$3,911	$4,353	$2,195
Mean International Airface												
(Number of Respondents)	24,359	661	1,426	339	146	204	23,662	624	1,514	319	134	159
Per Travel Party / Trip	$1,947	$1,448	$1,550	$1,617	$1,864	$2,380	$1,790	$1,490	$1,407	$1,684	$2,042	$2,027
Per Visitor / Trip	$1,315	$848	$904	$968	$1,197	$1,898	$1,222	$826	$835	$937	$1,110	$1,508
Mean Expenditure U.S. Airport												
(Number of Respondents)	31,614	940	1,977	480	191	244	31,609	923	2,097	476	184	191
Per Travel Party / Trip	$13	$18	$17	$22	$29	$12	$14	$15	$16	$16	$15	$14
Per Visitor / Trip	$8	$10	$9	$12	$17	$9	$9	$8	$9	$9	$7	$10
Mean Expenditure Outside U.S												
(Number of Respondents)	31,093	923	1.949	474	188	242	31,073	912	2,069	469	182	191
Per Travel Party / Trip	$1,933	$1,541	$2,076	$1,823	$1,786	$2,489	$1,796	$2,074	$2,214	$2,299	$3,458	$2,789
Per Visitor / Trip	$1,244	$860	$1,150	$1,023	$1,063	$1,930	$1,167	$1,097	$1,263	$1,225	$1,772	$2,036
Per Visitor / Day	$81	$53	$60	$52	$49	$73	$84	$66	$60	$61	$70	$77

YEAR - TO - DATE

Cross Tab 1
Section 4

US TRAVELERS TO OVERSEAS AND MEXICO
PRODUCED FOR ECO TOURISM INTERNATIONAL
JANUARY DECEMBER 1996 & 1999

TABLE 25

Q17. Trip Expenses Payment Method (%)

	Survey Year 1996						Survey Year 1999					
	US to Overseas	Leisure Env-Eco	Leisure Nati Prk	Lei/NP Env-Eco	Lei/NP Env/Camp	Business Env-Eco	US to Overseas	Leisure Env-Eco	Leisure Nati Prk	Lei/NP Env-Eco	Lei/NP Env/Camp	Business Env-Eco
(Number of Respondents)	30.694	913	1.957	478	191	237	31.325	943	2.133	473	183	201
Credit Cards	50.2	40.8	38.7	39.2	35.3	50.5	53.2	46.2	44.4	50.4	54.9	60.6
Travelers Checks	12.3	17.6	20.1	18.7	20.3	14.0	8.4	13.2	14.1	14.1	15.9	8.7
Debit Cards	1.6	2.1	3.1	2.3	4.3	1.0	3.9	4.5	6.0	4.3	4.8	3.9
Cash	35.9	39.6	38.1	39.8	40.2	34.6	34.6	36.1	35.5	31.2	24.4	26.8

YEAR - TO - DATE

US TRAVELERS TO OVERSEAS AND MEXICO
PRODUCED FOR ECO TOURISM INTERNATIONAL
JANUARY DECEMBER 1996 & 1999

TABLE 26 022b. Main Factor in Airline Choice (%)	Survey Year 1996						Survey Year 1999					
	US to Overseas	Leisure Env-Eco	Leisure Nati Prk	Lei/NP Env-Eco	Lei/NP Env/Camp	Business Env-Eco	US to Overseas	Leisure Env-Eco	Leisure Nati Prk	Lei/NP Env-Eco	Lei/NP Env/Camp	Business Env-Eco
(Number of Respondents)	22.466	593	1,364	320	134	174	22.271	608	1,490	337	145	132
Airface	22.3	33.7	30.3	37.4	42.7	20.7	25.7	28.3	36.5	25.3	25.8	15.1
Convenient Schedule	21.8	18.1	15.0	17.6	15.3	28.6	19.2	19.6	11.2	16.9	17.2	18.8
Employer Policy	3.1	0.4	0.3	0.5	1.2	5.5	3.7	1.3	1.2	1.5	2.2	5.4
In-Flight Svc. Rep.	2.0	3.5	3.3	4.1	7.9	2.3	1.4	1.7	1.5	3.5	7.1	1.6
Loyalty to Carrier	3.6	2.5	2.8	0.5	0.5	1.6	3.6	0.6	1.4	0.8	0.7	13.2
Mlg. Bonus / FF. Program	13.9	13.6	13.8	11.9	14.0	13.9	16.2	19.5	18.5	25.7	24.3	14.0
Non-Stop Flight	12.3	8.7	9.1	7.8	7.1	5.9	11.9	11.5	9.6	9.1	6.7	12.2
On-time Reputation	0.7	–	0.4	–	–	–	1.1	0.1	1.3	–	–	–
Prev. Good Experience	7.7	31	7.9	4.1	2.1	6.2	7.7	8.3	8.7	8.7	4.4	3.1
Safety Reputation	4.9	3.3	8.1	2.1	2.3	6.9	4.3	2.7	4.8	1.7	0.4	0.3
Other	7.6	13.0	9.1	14.0	6.8	8.6	5.1	6.5	5.4	6.8	11.2	16.3

YEAR - TO - DATE

Cross Tab 1
Section 5

US TRAVELERS TO OVERSEAS AND MEXICO
PRODUCED FOR ECO TOURISM INTERNATIONAL
JANUARY DECEMBER 1996 & 1999

TABLE 27

022a. Factor in Airline Choice* (%) (Number of Respondents)	Survey Year 1996						Survey Year 1999					
	US to Overseas	Leisure Env-Eco	Leisure Nati Prk	Lei/NP Env-Eco	Lei/NP Env/Camp	Business Env-Eco	US to Overseas	Leisure Env-Eco	Leisure Nati Prk	Lei/NP Env-Eco	Lei/NP Env/Camp	Business Env-Eco
	32,825	970	2,055	499	196	248	33,023	971	2,199	490	195	203
Not Involved in Choice	12.0	19.7	12.2	16.7	15.5	10.6	11.3	19.5	13.4	16.9	8.6	11.2
Involved in Choice	88.0	80.3	87.8	83.3	84.5	89.4	88.7	80.5	86.6	83.1	91.4	88.8
Airfare	36.5	42.0	43.4	44.2	49.3	36.7	39.9	39.5	47.3	38.9	44.7	33.8
Convenient Schedule	44.2	34.7	39.2	34.2	36.3	47.6	43.1	44.5	37.6	38.5	47.6	59.0
Employer Policy	4.5	0.6	1.2	0.6	1.5	9.0	5.0	0.9	1.4	1.0	1.5	7.3
In - Flight Svc. Rep	8.3	8.8	11.4	9.4	10.8	15.3	7.9	6.3	8.0	7.3	10.7	4.4
Loyalty to Carrier	10.2	6.7	9.6	7.6	4.2	11.3	10.2	6.5	8.4	10.2	8.9	20.7
Mlg. Bonus / FF. Program	28.2	22.2	22.9	22.9	20.8	29.9	29.2	27.6	28.2	33.9	35.7	37.3
Non - Stop Flight	31.9	24.7	30.4	26.9	33.9	27.1	30.1	27.0	29.0	26.6	29.0	31.0
On - time Reputation	5.8	4.4	6.0	5.5	7.9	4.4	5.5	1.6	6.3	2.5	2.8	3.2
Prev. Good Experience	26.2	18.7	25.9	15.9	12.0	24.6	25.2	19.1	23.9	21.8	23.6	11.5
Safety Reputation	14.6	12.7	20.0	14.2	22.6	12.9	12.8	10.7	14.2	10.1	5.6	4.3
Other	7.9	9.6	8.9	11.1	6.9	9.8	5.5	7.5	6.5	9.1	15.9	12.0

* Multiple Response. Based on top three choices in aggregate.

YEAR - TO - DATE

US TRAVELERS TO OVERSEAS AND MEXICO
PRODUCED FOR ECO TOURISM INTERNATIONAL
JANUARY DECEMBER 1996 & 1999

TABLE 28

Q23b. Type of Airline Ticket* (%)	Survey Year 1996						Survey Year 1999					
	US to Overseas	Leisure Env-Eco	Leisure Nati Prk	Lei/NP Env-Eco	Lei/NP Env/Camp	Business Env-Eco	US to Overseas	Leisure Env-Eco	Leisure Nati Prk	Lei/NP Env-Eco	Lei/NP Env/Camp	Business Env-Eco
(Number of Respondents)	34.291	1.017	2.153	521	210	258	34.374	1.009	2.305	508	195	209
Not Involved in Choice	12.0	19.7	12.2	16.7	15.5	10.6	11.3	19.5	13.4	16.9	8.6	11.2
First Class	5.8	2.3	2.8	2.5	2.2	7.4	4.6	5.2	3.5	2.5	0.5	2.2
Executive / Business	15.2	4.2	5.5	2.9	2.8	23.3	13.8	5.0	4.9	6.9	8.7	24.0
Economy / Tourist / Coach	68.3	76.1	78.9	77.5	76.6	53.0	69.8	74.8	77.8	76.0	80.7	60.8
Frequent Flyer Award	5.7	7.6	7.4	6.5	5.8	7.0	6.8	8.6	7.6	8.0	8.9	4.8
Frequent Flyer Upgrade	3.9	1.8	2.6	2.4	2.4	7.3	4.4	2.5	4.3	3.0	2.3	3.8
Discount / Group Fare	3.5	6.7	4.4	6.6	6.6	8.8	2.9	3.0	3.4	2.3	1.6	2.9
Non - Revenue	2.3	2.0	2.2	1.1	0.2	5.6	2.8	2.8	2.0	4.2	5.0	2.0
Dont Know	2.8	45	35	4.9	7.3	2.2	2.3	3.9	2.0	2.8	0.7	4.1

* Multiple Response.

YEAR - TO - DATE

Cross Tab 1
Section 5

US TRAVELERS TO OVERSEAS AND MEXICO
PRODUCED FOR ECO TOURISM INTERNATIONAL
JANUARY DECEMBER 1996 & 1999

TABLE 29

Q23a. Seating Area (%)	Survey Year 1996					Survey Year 1999				
	US to Overseas	Leisure Env-Eco	Leisure Nati Prk	Lei/NP Env-Eco	Lei/NP Env/Camp	Business Env-Eco	US to Overseas	Leisure Env-Eco	Leisure Nati Prk	Lei/NP Env-Eco	Lei/NP Env/Camp	Business Env-Eco
(Number of Respondents)	34,343	1.018	2,153	518	207	258	34.398	1,007	2.310	514	197	208
First Class	9.3	5.6	4.3	4.3	3.8	13.9	6.8	7.1	4.2	3.9	3.0	12.3
Executive / Business	17.4	6.1	9.0	5.1	3.3	27.2	17.9	8.4	11.4	10.9	12.3	22.5
Economy / Tourist / Coach	73.3	88.3	86.7	90.6	92.9	58.9	75.2	84.5	84.4	85.2	84.7	65.2

YEAR - TO - DATE

Cross Tab 1
Section 6

US TRAVELERS TO OVERSEAS AND MEXICO
PRODUCED FOR ECO TOURISM INTERNATIONAL
JANUARY DECEMBER 1996 & 1999

TABLE 30

Q28b. Sex & Age of Traveler (%)	Survey Year 1996						Survey Year 1999					
	US to Overseas	Leisure Env-Eco	Leisure Nati Prk	Lei/NP Env-Eco	Lei/NP Env/Camp	Business Env-Eco	US to Overseas	Leisure Env-Eco	Leisure Nati Prk	Lei/NP Env-Eco	Lei/NP Env/Camp	Business Env-Eco
(Number of Respondents)	32,118	943	1,995	479	192	249	31,950	931	2,135	467	183	199
Male Adults	62.6	50.4	53.7	54.9	60.6	75.7	59.9	54.2	52.3	46.5	44.1	74.6
18 - 24 Years	2.7	32.6	4.4	5.5	5.7	1.6	3.2	4.2	3.3	3.0	6.2	2.7
25 - 29 Years	4.8	6.4	6.8	7.6	14.9	1.3	5.1	5.5	5.4	5.9	4.6	5.1
30 - 34 Years	6.9	6.5	7.5	8.2	9.9	9.6	6.5	6.9	5.3	3.5	4.6	5.0
35 - 39 Years	8.1	5.4	5.5	5.8	2.5	6.4	7.9	5.9	8.1	4.0	4.6	7.7
40 - 44 Years	8.9	5.0	5.1	4.7	5.9	9.2	7.9	6.1	4.9	4.0	3.1	5.5
45 - 49 Years	8.9	6.1	6.9	7.2	13.5	13.4	7.3	5.9	3.7	4.1	3.0	9.1
50 - 54 Years	7.5	5.9	4.6	5.6	3.2	13.4	7.5	7.5	5.1	8.3	11.0	19.9
55 - 64 Years	9.0	4.5	6.0	3.3	2.3	18.1	9.3	7.9	7.4	8.5	6.4	17.1
65 + Years	5.8	7.0	6.9	7.1	2.7	2.8	5.3	4.3	9.0	5.2	0.5	2.5
Mean Male Age	45.1	43.9	43.5	42.1	38.1	47.4	44.9	43.7	46.0	46.2	41.6	46.7
Median Male Age	44.0	43.0	41.0	40.0	34.0	48.0	44.0	43.0	43.0	48.0	42.0	50.0
Female Adults	37.4	49.6	46.3	45.1	39.4	24.3	40.1	45.8	47.7	53.5	55.9	25.4
18 - 24 Years	3.1	3.1	4.1	3.4	5.6	0.2	3.8	4.0	4.6	4.1	7.0	0.5
25 - 29 Years	4.3	3.9	4.4	3.9	3.7	2.1	4.7	7.7	6.0	7.0	6.2	3.3
30 - 34 Years	4.9	5.5	8.2	3.3	3.3	4.2	5.0	5.5	5.3	6.0	3.2	7.7
35 - 39 Years	5.0	7.1	4.6	4.9	4.2	3.3	4.9	3.6	5.4	4.8	3.7	2.5
40 - 44 Years	4.7	7.4	5.5	6.7	3.5	6.5	5.2	2.6	6.0	2.7	3.8	1.3
45 - 49 Years	4.6	5.3	4.6	6.7	6.1	3.7	4.1	4.9	5.1	6.3	9.1	4.1
50 - 54 Years	3.6	5.7	4.9	6.1	3.1	2.9	4.2	5.8	5.2	6.4	5.2	2.1
55 - 64 Years	4.4	8.5	6.6	8.3	8.7	1.3	5.3	8.5	6.5	12.6	16.1	3.0
65 + Years	2.8	3.0	3.5	1.7	1.3	0.2	2.9	3.4	3.7	3.6	1.6	1.0
Mean Female Age	42.1	43.5	42.4	43.3	41.5	41.3	42.3	42.9	42.6	44.2	43.0	40.1
Median Female Age	41.0	44.0	43.0	45.0	43.0	43.0	41.0	43.0	42.0	45.0	45.0	35.0

YEAR - TO - DATE

Cross Tab 1
Section 6

US TRAVELERS TO OVERSEAS AND MEXICO
PRODUCED FOR ECO TOURISM INTERNATIONAL
JANUARY DECEMBER 1996 & 1999

TABLE 31

Q28a. Occupation (%)

	Survey Year 1996						Survey Year 1999					
	US to Overseas	Leisure Env-Eco	Leisure Nati Prk	Lei/NP Env-Eco	Lei/NP Env/Camp	Business Env-Eco	US to Overseas	Leisure Env-Eco	Leisure Nati Prk	Lei/NP Env-Eco	Lei/NP Env/Camp	Business Env-Eco
(Number of Respondents)	33,478	991	2,092	502	204	258	33,506	965	2,238	490	189	204
Clerical / Sales	5.5	4.7	8.4	4.8	4.0	3.0	5.3	7.1	5.2	6.1	1.9	1.0
Craftsman / Factory Worker	3.6	1.8	5.7	2.1	2.4	1.3	3.4	4.1	4.4	2.9	3.1	0.3
Government / Military	2.2	3.4	3.2	2.3	5.1	0.8	1.9	2.0	2.0	2.5	3.6	0.7
Homemaker	4.9	5.6	4.3	2.2	2.8	–	5.6	3.6	6.7	5.4	9.1	–
Manager / Executive	32.4	24.2	21.1	24.5	22.6	43.8	29.7	19.8	17.9	20.8	22.9	32.4
Professional / Technical	36.8	41.6	34.5	39.1	42.5	41.6	37.7	42.4	39.1	40.1	42.3	63.1
Retired	8.7	10.0	13.1	11.8	6.3	2.6	9.6	12.8	15.0	14.6	5.7	0.5
Student	4.9	8.2	8.8	12.7	13.7	5.5	5.9	7.6	8.1	7.0	11.0	1.6
Other	0.9	0.5	0.9	0.3	0.5	1.4	0.8	0.6	1.5	0.6	0.4	0.4

YEAR - TO - DATE

Cross Tab 1
Section 6

US TRAVELERS TO OVERSEAS AND MEXICO
PRODUCED FOR ECO TOURISM INTERNATIONAL
JANUARY DECEMBER 1996 & 1999

TABLE 32

Q29. Annual Household Income (%)	Survey Year 1996						Survey Year 1999					
	US to Overseas	Leisure Env-Eco	Leisure Nati Prk	Lei/NP Env-Eco	Lei/NP Env/Camp	Business Env-Eco	US to Overseas	Leisure Env-Eco	Leisure Nati Prk	Lei/NP Env-Eco	Lei/NP Env/Camp	Business Env-Eco
(Number of Respondents)	30.850	907	1.923	460	186	248	30.395	888	2,059	447	181	187
Under $20.000	4.9	5.1	7.9	7.4	4.7	8.4	4.1	3.0	5.9	3.5	4.0	0.8
$20.000 - $39999	12.8	15.1	18.4	15.7	11.0	7.5	10.8	7.8	14.2	8.0	4.6	7.4
$40.000 - $59,999	16.3	20.1	17.9	16.8	17.1	9.1	15.4	14.4	19.8	15.0	12.0	11.9
$60,000 - $79,999	15.1	18.2	17.8	19.7	20.3	13.5	13.8	19.2	11.7	13.0	7.5	21.5
$80,000 - $99,999	12.2	10.6	12.4	10.6	9.2	13.1	12.3	12.7	14.1	12.0	19.6	13.7
$100,000 - $119,999	9.8	9.1	7.6	11.2	17.1	14.7	10.9	9.8	9.7	9.1	7.6	7.6
$120,000 - $139,999	6.6	4.3	3.7	3.6	2.0	14.0	6.6	6.8	4.4	7.8	8.8	7.6
$140,000 - $159,999	4.9	4.5	3.5	0.8	0.6	4.2	5.2	4.6	4.2	5.0	6.9	9.4
$160,000 - $179,999	2.5	2.9	2.0	4.7	6.9	0.9	3.2	1.1	1.5	1.0	0.5	2.3
$180,000 - $199,999	2.0	1.9	1.8	1.6	1.6	1.1	2.5	0.6	0.7	0.6	0.1	2.7
$200,000 and over	12.9	8.4	6.9	8.0	9.4	12.7	15.3	20.0	13.8	24.8	28.6	15.1
Mean Annual Income	$96.000	$85,600	$78,800	$83,000	$91,700	$100,200	$102,600	$108,200	$91,100	$112,900	$121,600	$108,900
Median Annual Income	$81,500	$70,700	$66,500	$70,300	$76,900	$96.400	$89.50	$88,600	$77,100	$97,300	$106,100	$92,400

Annex B

U.S. DEPARTMENT OF COMMERCE
INTERNATIONAL TRADE ADMINISTRATION
Tourism Industries

SURVEY OF INTERNATIONAL AIR TRAVELERS

DEPARTING THE UNITED STATES

Dear International Traveler:

Please help the travel industry improve the services they offer you. The information collected in this survey is used by airlines, travel agents, hotels, government travel offices, and other travel planners and providers to understand you, the international traveler, and thereby take steps to help improve your next international trip.

This questionnaire is designed to be completed by both non-U.S. residents who have visited the country and U.S. residents traveling abroad. If you are 18 years of age or older, please complete this voluntary survey. **ONLY ONE RESPONSE PER FAMILY GROUP, PLEASE.**

Upon completing this survey, please return it to the person who provided it to you. The estimated average time to complete this questionnaire is 15 minutes. Should you have any comments regarding this survey, please send them to the Tourism Industries, ITA, Washington, DC 20230, or the Office of Information and Regulatory Affairs, OMB, Project 0625-0227,Washington, DC 20503.

Thank you for your cooperation on this important survey.

إستطلاع آراء هذا سنوفر إيضا بقتلة العربية. تقضل بطلب نسخة منه إذا شئت

本調查表備有中文版。歡迎索取
Questionnaire disponible en français. Veuillez le réclamer s'il vous plaît.
Diese Umfrage ist auch auf deutsch erhältlich. Bei Bedarf bitte ein Exemplar anfordern.
Questa indagine è disponibile anche in italiano. Se necessario, si prega di richiederne una copia.
本アンケートには日本語版も用意してあります。 他のものにお申しつけください。
한국말로 된 설문서도 있습니다. 개원에게 요청하십시오.
Ta ankieta jest także na żadanie dostępna po polsku.
Ha uma versão em Português da presente pesquisa. Se for necessário, favor pedir uma cópia.
Данный вопросник также имеется на русском языке. Пожалуйста, попросите русскоязычный экземпляр
Este cuestionario también está en español. Solicítelo.

OMB No. 0625-0227 Expires: 9/30/98

 World Tourism Organization

Page 2

ONLY ONE RESPONSE PER FAMILY, PLEASE.

Month   Day   Year

1a. Date ————————►

b. Name of airline ————————►

c. Flight number ————————►

d. Please rate your general impression of this airline.
Mark (X) ONE

5 ☐ Excellent
4 ☐ Good
3 ☐ Average
2 ☐ Fair
1 ☐ Poor

2a. What are your City, State, ZIP (postal) Code, and Country of RESIDENCE? — Specify ↗

City

State   ZIP (Postal) Code

Country

Non-U.S. Residents — SKIP to question 2c.

b. If this flight is part of an outbound journey from your home, what will be the main destination on your trip? — Specify ↗

Destination

c. For Non-U.S. Residents ONLY
If this flight is part of the return journey to your home, what was the main destination that you visited since you left home? — Specify ↗

Destination

3a. What is your country of CITIZENSHIP? — Specify ↗

b. What is your country of BIRTH? — Specify ↗

U.S. Residents — SKIP to question 4b.

4a. For Non-U.S. Residents ONLY
At what city or airport did you pass through U.S. Customs/Immigration? — Specify ↗

Non-U.S. Residents — SKIP to question 5a.

4b. If you are a U.S. resident, at what city or airport will you pass through U.S. Customs/Immigration when you return? — Specify ↗

5a. At which airport did or will you board this aircraft today? — Specify ↗

b. Did you make a connecting flight?
2 ☐ No
1 ☐ Yes — From which airport? — Specify ↗

c. At which airport will you leave this aircraft? — Specify ↗

d. Once there, are you making a connecting flight?
2 ☐ No
1 ☐ Yes — To which city? — Specify ↗

6. How did you obtain the information used to plan your trip?
Mark (X) ALL that apply

☐ Airlines directly
☐ In-flight information systems
☐ National government tourist office
☐ State/City travel office
☐ Friends or relatives
☐ Travel agency
☐ Travel guides
☐ Tour company
☐ Corporate travel department
☐ Newspapers/Magazines
☐ TV/Radio
☐ Personal computer

7. How long before you departed on this trip did you —

Days

Decide to travel? ————————►

Days

Make the airline reservations? ————————►

8. How were your AIRLINE reservations for this trip made?
Mark (X) ONE

1 ☐ A travel agent
2 ☐ A travel club
3 ☐ The airline directly
4 ☐ The company's travel department
5 ☐ Tour operator
6 ☐ Personal computer
7 ☐ Don't know
8 ☐ Other

CONTINUE WITH QUESTION 9 ON PAGE 3.

9a. Were commercial LODGING reservations made for this trip before you left home?
Mark (X) ONE
1 ☐ Yes — *Go to question 9b*
2 ☐ No — *SKIP to question 10a*

b. These reservations were made through …
Mark (X) ALL that apply
1 ☐ A travel agent
2 ☐ The hotel/motel staff directly
3 ☐ The company's travel department
4 ☐ A tour operator
5 ☐ Airline staff
6 ☐ A friend or relative
7 ☐ Business associate
8 ☐ Other

10a. What is/was the MAIN purpose of your trip?
Mark (X) ONE
1 ☐ Business/Professional
2 ☐ Convention/Conference/Trade show
3 ☐ Leisure/Recreation/Holidays/Sightseeing
4 ☐ Visit friends/Relatives
5 ☐ Government affairs/Military
6 ☐ Study/Teaching
7 ☐ Religion/Pilgrimages
8 ☐ Health treatment
9 ☐ Other — *Specify* ↗

CONTINUE WITH QUESTION 10b.

10b. Does this trip have any other purposes?
Mark (X) ALL that apply
1 ☐ Business/Professional
2 ☐ Convention/Conference/Trade show
3 ☐ Leisure/Recreation/Holidays/Sightseeing
4 ☐ Visit friends/Relatives
5 ☐ Government affairs/Military
6 ☐ Study/Teaching
7 ☐ Religion/Pilgrimages
8 ☐ Health treatment
9 ☐ Other — *Specify* ↗

11. With whom are you traveling now?
Mark (X) ALL that apply
1 ☐ Spouse
2 ☐ Family/Relative
3 ☐ Business associate(s)
4 ☐ Friend(s)
5 ☐ Tour group
6 ☐ Traveling alone

12. Altogether, how many adults and/or children are in your travel party? Exclude your tour group members unless you knew them and planned to travel with them prior to booking the tour.

Number of adults ―――――――――▸

Number of children
under 18 years old ―――――――▸

13. How many nights away from home will you spend or have you spent on this trip?

Number of nights in the USA
(including U.S. territories) ―――――▸

Number of nights outside the USA ――▸

14. IN ORDER OF VISIT, list the principal places visited or to be visited on this trip, and indicate the number of nights at each place. Under number of nights, if you did not or will not stay overnight at a place visited, enter "0". Under the section for type of lodging, indicate the lodging company name, or mark (X) in the appropriate space.

Destinations (Cities/Attractions) Enter ONLY ONE destination per line	State or Country	Number of nights	Type of lodging Select ONE per line		
			Hotel/Motel Specify name of company	Mark (X)	
				Private home	Other
1					
2					
3					
4					
5					
6					
7					

CONTINUE WITH QUESTION 15 ON PAGE 4.

Page 4

15a. Is this trip part of a package? *Mark (X) ONE*

2 ☐ No — *SKIP to question 16*

1 ☐ Yes — **Which of the following does your package include?**
Mark (X) ALL that apply

     1 ☐ Airfare
     2 ☐ Rental car
     3 ☐ Tour escort for entire trip
     2 ☐ Cruise
     5 ☐ Intercity bus/Coach transportation
     6 ☐ Commercial guided tours
     7 ☐ Commercial lodging — **How many nights lodging are included?** ————————➤

b. How many days prior to departure was this package booked? — *Specify* ————————➤

c. What is the approximate cost of your prepaid package?
Please give your answer in U.S. dollars or your own country's currency ————————➤

IF OTHER THAN U.S. CURRENCY ————————
specify country of currency used. ————————➤

16. About your trip expenditures...please estimate the amount of money spent, or expected to be spent for the following items. Please remember your name is not on this form. Your cooperation in completing this important question is appreciated.

a. Please estimate how much money you spent, or will spend, outside your own country. Do not include those items which were covered in the package mentioned in 15c above. — *Specify* ———➤

b. Country of currency used for estimate — *Specify* ————————➤

c. How many people are covered by this expenditure estimate?
Specify total number of people ————————➤

d. What was the total cost of your international air travel tickets? — *Specify* ————————➤

     ☐ *Mark (X) here if you do NOT know cost of tickets.*

e. Are these ONE WAY tickets?
Mark (X) ONE
     1 ☐ Yes
     2 ☐ No

f. How much did you spend at the airport of your USA departure? — *Specify* ————————➤

U.S. Residents — *SKIP to question 17.*

For Non-U.S. Residents ONLY

g. Of the total expenditure given in 16a,
please estimate how much was spent in the USA. — *Specify* ————————➤

h. Of the total expenditure given in 16g above, **please estimate how much was for—**

     1. Transportation ————————➤

     2. Lodging ————————➤

     3. Foods and beverages ————————➤

     4. Gifts, souvenirs and other purchases ————————➤

     5. Entertainment and recreation ————————➤

     6. Other spending (if any) ————————➤

CONTINUE WITH QUESTION 17 ON PAGE 5.

17. Please tell us about how you did, or will, pay for your expenses on this trip —

Type of payment	Percentage paid for expenses	Company(ies) of issue
Credit card(s)	%	
Travelers check(s)	%	
Debit card(s)	%	
Cash	%	
TOTAL	100 %	

8. What types of transportation did you, or will you, use when reaching your destination on this trip?

Mark (X) ALL that apply

- Airlines within the USA
- Airlines outside the USA
- Railroad between cities
- Rented auto — *Specify company name* ↗

- Taxi/Cab/Limousine
- City subway/Tram/Bus
- Bus between cities
- Company or private auto
- Motor home/Camper

9. Which of the following leisure activities did you, or will you, spend time on during this trip?

Mark (X) ALL that apply

- Shopping
- Dining in restaurants
- Amusement/Theme parks
- Visiting historical places
- Visiting casinos/Gambling
- Commercial guided tours
- Visiting small towns and villages
- Cultural heritage sights/Activities
- Touring the countryside
- Water sports/Sunbathing
- Ranch vacations
- Cruises
- Hunting/Fishing
- Snow skiing
- Golfing/Tennis
- Camping/Hiking
- Environmental/Ecological excursions
- Visiting national parks
- Visiting American Indian communities
- Attending sports event
- Concert/Play/Musical
- Art gallery/Museum
- Sightseeing in cities
- Nightclubs/Dancing
- Ethnic heritage sights/Activities

CONTINUE WITH QUESTION 20 ON PAGE 6.

Page 6

20. **Please rate this airline for this trip on each of the following attributes.**
Mark (X) ONE rating

	Excellent	Good	Average	Fair	Poor	Did Not Use
a. Convenient schedule						
b. Ticket price						
c. Reservation service						
d. Check-in waiting time						
e. Check-in personnel						
f. Airline club/Lounge						
g. On-time departure						
h. Food/Beverage quality						
i. Flight attendant service						
j. Audio/Video						
k. Cabin cleanliness						
l. Cabin noise level						
m. Seat comfort						
n. Cabin layout						
o. Carry-on storage space						
p. Overall evaluation of aircraft						
q. Overall evaluation of flight						

21. **Would you choose or recommend this airline for your next trip on this route?**
Mark (X) ONE
- Definitely would
- Probably would
- Probably would not
- Definitely would not
- Not sure

22. **What were your three main reasons for flying on THIS AIRLINE?** Indicate by marking "1" for the most important reason, "2" for the next most important reason, and "3" for the third most important reason. DO NOT indicate more than three reasons.

- Airfare
- Convenient schedule
- Non-stop flights
- Employer policy
- Safety reputation
- Loyalty to carrier

- On-time reputation
- Previous good experience
- Mileage bonus/Frequent flyer program
- In-flight service reputation
- Not involved in choice of carrier
- Other — *specify* ⟳

23a. **Where are you sitting today?**
Mark (X) ONE
- First class
- Executive/Business class
- Economy/Tourist/Coach

b. **What type of airline ticket do you have?**
Mark (X) ALL that apply
- First class
- Executive/Business class
- Economy/Tourist/Coach
- Frequent flyer free ticket

- Frequent flyer upgrade
- Discount/Group fare
- Non-revenue
- Don't know

CONTINUE WITH QUESTION 24 ON PAGE 7.

Page 7

24. Please rate the following attributes of the AIRPORT from which you have just departed (or are currently waiting to depart) the United States.

Mark (X) ONE rating for each

	Excellent	Good	Average	Fair	Poor	Did Not Use
a. Airport access	☐	☐	☐	☐	☐	☐
b. Ground transportation	☐	☐	☐	☐	☐	☐
c. Airport terminal convenience	☐	☐	☐	☐	☐	☐
d. Airport terminal cleanliness	☐	☐	☐	☐	☐	☐
e. Concession goods/Services	☐	☐	☐	☐	☐	☐
f. Concession prices	☐	☐	☐	☐	☐	☐
g. Terminal seating availability	☐	☐	☐	☐	☐	☐
h. International traveller facilities	☐	☐	☐	☐	☐	☐
i. Security measures	☐	☐	☐	☐	☐	☐
j. Overall airport evaluation	☐	☐	☐	☐	☐	☐

U.S. Residents — SKIP to question 26a

25a. For Non-U.S. Residents ONLY

When entering the USA, please rate your Immigration and Naturalization Service/Passport Control and U.S. Customs experience at the airport where you entered the USA.

Mark (X) ONE rating for each

	Excellent	Good	Average	Fair	Poor	Don't know
a. Passport control						
(1) Processing time	☐	☐	☐	☐	☐	☐
(2) Staff courtesy	☐	☐	☐	☐	☐	☐
b. Customs baggage clearance						
(1) Processing time	☐	☐	☐	☐	☐	☐
(2) Staff courtesy	☐	☐	☐	☐	☐	☐

b. About how long did it take you to clear Passport Control and Customs when entering the United States?

Specify in minutes 7

c. Baggage delivery waiting time

Mark (X) ONE rating

- ☐ Excellent
- ☐ Good
- ☐ Average
- ☐ Fair
- ☐ Poor
- ☐ Don't know

26a. Did you have personal safety concerns before you started your international trip?

Mark (X) ONE

- ☐ Yes
- ☐ No

b. Did your concerns cause you to change your travel plans?

Mark (X) ONE

- ☐ Yes
- ☐ No

• **U.S. Residents** — SKIP to question 27a.
• **Non-U.S. Residents** — Continue with question 26c on page 8

Page 8

26c. For Non-U.S. Residents ONLY

Was your personal safety actually endangered while in the USA?

Mark (X) ONE

☐ No — *Go to question 27*

☐ Yes — *Indicate the city(ies) where incident(s) took place and mark (X) the appropriate category(ies) below.* ➤

City	Incidents — Mark (X)					
	Harassment/ Arguments	Assault/ Physical Harm	Burglary/ Theft	Transportation accident	Health problem	Other—Specify

27a. **Is this your first trip by air to/from the United States?**

Mark (X) ONE

☐ Yes — *SKIP to question 28*

☐ No — *Go to question 27b*

b. **Altogether, how many round trips by air have you made to/from the United States—**

In the past 12 months? ————————————————➤

In the past 5 years? ————————————————➤

28. **Please give us some information about yourself.**

a. **What is your occupation?**

Mark (X) ONE

☐ Manager/Executive

☐ Professional/Technical

☐ Clerical/Sales

☐ Craftsman/Mechanic/Factory worker

☐ Government/Military

☐ Homemaker

☐ Retired

☐ Student

☐ Other — *Specify* ➤

b. **Age** ————————➤

c. **Gender**— *Mark (X) ONE*

☐ Female

☐ Male

29. **What is the total combined yearly income of all members of your household?** *Give your answer either in USA dollars or in your own country's currency. Please specify the country of currency if NOT USA dollars.*

In USA dollars —

Mark (X) ONE

☐ Under $20,000

☐ $20,000-$39,999

☐ $40,000-$59,999

☐ $60,000-$79,999

☐ $80,000-$99,999

☐ $100,000-$119,999

☐ $120,000-$139,999

☐ $140,000-$159,999

☐ $160,000-$179,999

☐ $180,000-$199,999

☐ $200,000 and above

OR

In currency other than USA dollars— *Specify* ➤

Total annual household income ————➤

Country of currency ————➤

THANK YOU FOR COMPLETING THIS QUESTIONNAIRE.
WE HOPE YOUR TRIP WAS OR WILL BE AN ENJOYABLE ONE.

Annex C

WTO STUDY TOUR OPERATOR QUESTIONNAIRE

1. The WTO would like to know what you consider to be the essential elements of ecotourism. (please circle, ranked on a score of 1-5, with 1 being most important)

a. All forms of nature-based tourism in which the main motivation of tourists is:
   - the observation and appreciation of nature, 1 2 3 4 5
   - the traditional cultures prevailing in natural areas, 1 2 3 4 5

b. It minimizes negative impacts on the natural and socio-cultural environment,
   1 2 3 4 5

c. It actively promotes conservation through financial or other support, 1 2 3 4 5

d. It emphasizes generation of economic benefits to local communities, 1 2 3 4 5

e. It contains significant educational and interpretive features, 1 2 3 4 5

2. Please indicate the approximate proportion of your business that is ecotourism.
   Less than 10% ( ), 11-25% ( ), 26-50% ( ), 51-75% ( ), 76-90% ( ), over 90% ( )

3. Over the past five years, has the proportion of clients that your company carried on ecotourism programs remained relatively constant ( ) increased ( ) or decreased ( )? By approximately what percentage per year ____?

4. Do you anticipate that ecotourism will be an increasing ( ), decreasing ( ), or relatively constant ( ) proportion of your business over the next five years?

5. Approximately what percent of your ecotourism business is foreign inbound (___ %), U.S. domestic (____ %), and U.S. outbound (____ %)

6. Do you use the concept of ecotourism in promoting your company? Yes ( ) No ( )

7. Do you have specific programs to (give examples if possible):
   a. minimize adverse visitor impacts on the environment?   Yes ( )   No ( )
   b. encourage clients to contribute ($ or time) to conservation?   Yes ( )   No ( )
   c. encourage a greater understanding of the natural environment? Yes ( )   No ( )
   d. promote the economic well-being of local communities?   Yes ( )   No ( )

Examples:_____
_____
_____
_____

8. Do you think that your ecotourism clients would be willing to pay a premium if they were confident that ecotourism criteria were being followed: Yes ( ) No ( ) ? If so, would they be willing to pay 0-5% ( ), 5-10% ( ), or over 10% ( ) more?

9. Would you characterize your trips as primarily aimed at:

Budget travel ( )
Mid-level travel ( )
High-end or luxury travel ( )

10. What percent of your trips would you characterize as:

Pure ecotourism (___%)
Mixed travel (e.g., nature and heritage/culture/adventure/sightseeing) (___%)
Travel in which ecotourism is clearly secondary (___%)

11. What are the priorities of your clients in choosing a destination (1 is highest priority)?

Being in wilderness areas	1 2 3 4 5
Viewing wildlife	1 2 3 4 5
Birdwatching	1 2 3 4 5
Seeing rare species	1 2 3 4 5
Botany	1 2 3 4 5
Geology	1 2 3 4 5
Marine/water attractions	1 2 3 4 5
Archeology/cultural attractions	1 2 3 4 5
Meeting indigenous people	1 2 3 4 5
Relaxation	1 2 3 4 5
Sports/adventure	1 2 3 4 5
Education/learning	1 2 3 4 5
Contribute to conservation	1 2 3 4 5
High quality accommodations	1 2 3 4 5
High quality food	1 2 3 4 5
Excellent local guides	1 2 3 4 5
Small groups	1 2 3 4 5
Uncrowded areas	1 2 3 4 5
Low overall cost of trip	1 2 3 4 5

12. For your primary destinations, could you guess approximately what proportion of travelers are fully independent travelers (FITs) versus groups? FITs (___%) versus groups (___%)

13. Do you believe that the proportion of FITs is increasing (   ), decreasing (   ), or staying about the same (   )

14. Which marketing channels are most useful to you (please circle, rank 1 as highest)?

Catalogues	1 2 3 4 5
Brochures	1 2 3 4 5
Mailings	1 2 3 4 5
Advertisements	1 2 3 4 5
Internet	1 2 3 4 5
Word-of-mouth	1 2 3 4 5
Affinity group	1 2 3 4 5
Travel agents	1 2 3 4 5

15. Are National Travel Office useful to you marketing of ecotourism? Yes ( ) No ( ) If so, please explain what is most helpful

_____

_____

Thank you very much for you assistance.

Please check if you would like a copy of the report when it is available. Yes ( ) No ( )
Name, company and mailing address:

_____

_____

_____

_____

Annex D

SELECTED CONTACT INFORMATION
U.S. ECOTOURISM ORGANIZATIONS

Adventure Travel Society
228 North F Street
Salida, CO 81201
719-530-0171
www.adventuretravel.com

American Society of Travel Agents (ASTA)
1101 King Street, Suite 200
Alexandria, VA 22314
703-73—2782
www.astanet.com

National Tour Association (NTA)
546 East Main Street,
Lexington, Kentucky 40508
859-226-4444
www.ntaonline.com

The International Adventure Travel and Outdoor Show (IATOS)
World Congress on Adventure and Eco Tourism
Chicago, Illinois
877-604-2867
iatos@msemgmt.com

The International Ecotourism Society (TIES)
P.O Box 668
Burlington, VT 05402
802-651-9818
www.ecotourism.org

U.S. TOUR OPERATORS LIST
(Members of The International Ecotourism Society)

Abercrombie & Kent
9301Nmorth A1A, Suite 1
Vero Beach, FL 32963
800-323-7308
jwebley@abercrombiekent.com

Absorbtours, Inc.
545 8th Ave., 18th Floor
New York, NY 10018
877-277-6728
rcb@absorbtours.com

Alaska Wildland Adventures
PO Box 389
Girdwood, AK 99587
800-334-8730
info@alaskawildland.com

Amazonia Expeditions, Inc.
10305 Riverburn Dr.
Tampa, FL 33647
800-262-9669
paul.beaver@gte.net

Angel-Eco Tours, Inc.
53 Remsen Street, Suite 6
Brooklyn, NY 11201
212-656-1240
stanley@angel-ecotours.com

Annette's Adventures
45-403 Koa Kahiko St.
Kaneohe, HI
808-235-5431
annettesadventures@juno.com

Asia Transpacific Journeys
2995 Center Green Court
Boulder, CO 80301
303-443-6789
travel@southeastasia.com

Backroads
801 Cedar Street
Berkley, CA 94710
800-462-2848
tomh@backroads.com

Bridge Travel Alliance
2200 Powell St., Suite 130
Emeryville. CA 94608
510-496-8275
karenk@escapeartists.com

Caligo Ventures
156 Bedford Rd.
Armonk, NY 10504
800-462-2848
info@caligo.com

Cheeseman's Ecology Safaris
20800 Kittredge Road
Saratoga, CA 95070
408-741-5330
cheesemans@aol.com

Classic Journeys
5580 La Jolla Blev, Suite 104
La Jolla, CA 92037
619-454-5004
edward@classicjourneys.com

Costa Rica Connection
1124 Nipomo Street, Suite C
San Luis Obispo, CA 93401
805-543-8823
tours@cronnect.com

Columbus Travel
900 Ridge Creek Lane
Bulverde, TX 78163
800-843-1060

Country Walkers
PO Box 180
Waterbury, VT 05676
800-464-9255
info@countrywalkers.com

Desert Paths Tours
2537 E. Richards Place
Tucson, AZ 85716
520-327-7235
lcooper@desertpaths.com

Dreamweaver Travel
1185 River Drive
River Falls, WI 54022
715-425-1037
dudley@dreamweavertravel.com

East Quest
1 Union Square W, Suite 606
New York, NY 10003
212-741-1688
eastquest1@aol.com

EcoSouthwest.com
PO Box 213
Blue Diamond, NV 89004
877-474-8492
r.holtzin@att.net

Ecotours International, Inc.
PO Box 1853
Pebble Beach, CA 93953
831-625-3135
bforeman@redshift.com

Edutreks
751 White Oak Road
Boone, NC 28607
828-963-7407
john@edutreks.com

Focus Tours, Inc.
103 Moya Road
Sante Fe, NM 87505
505-466-4688
FocusTours@aol.com

Hawaii Forest and Trail, Ltd.
74-5035B   Queen   Kaahumanu
Highway
Kailua-Kona HI 96740
808-331-8505
rob@hawaii-forest.com

Homosassa Kayaking Company
5300 South Cherokee Way
Homosassa, FL 34448
352-628-3183
cedav53@extalwind.net

International Expeditions
One Environs Park
Helena, AL 35080
800-633-4734
rryel@ietravel.com

J.B. Starkey's Flatwoods Adventures
12959 S>R> 54
Odessa, FL 33556
813-926-1133
flatwoods@earthlink.net

Journey's International, Inc.
107 April Drive, Suite 3
Ann Arbor, MI 48103
734-665-4407
info@journeys-intl.com

Lindblad Special Expeditions
1415 Western Ave., Suite 700
Seattle, WA 98101
800-527-6298
travel@specialexpeditions.com

Manaca, Inc.
1609 Connecticut Ave. NW, 4th Floor
Washington DC 20009
202-265-8204
andreas@manaca.com

MaupinAdventures
1421 Research Park Drive, Suite 300
P.O. Box 807
Lawrence, KS 66049
785-331-1070
ngolden@maupintour.com

Mountain Travel Sobek
6420 Fairmont Ave.
El Cerrito, CA 94530
888-687-6235
info@mtsobek.com

Myths and Mountains
976 Tee Court
Incline Village, NV 89541
775-832-5454
travel@mythsandmountains.com

Natural Habitat Adventures
2945 Center Green Ct., Suite H
Boulder, CO 80301
800-543-8917
nathab@worldnet.att.net

Nature Discoveries
PO Box 427
Rochester, NY 14603
716-473-1098
sdaniel1@rochester.rr.com

Nature Expeditions
7860 Peters Road, Suite F-103
Plantation, FL 33324
954-693-8852
NaturExp@aol.com

Ozark Ecotours
PO Box 513
Jasper, AK 72641
870-446-5898
ncrx@jasper.yournet.com

Nomadic Expeditions
1095 Cranbury South River Rd.,
Suite 20A
Jamesburg, NJ 08831
609-860-9008
info@nomadicexpeditions.com

Orchids and Egrets Florida Eco-Tours
238 Silverado Dr.
Naples, FL 34119
941-352-8586
ecotour@peganet.com

Overseas Adventure Travel
1 Broadway, Suite 600
Cambridge, MA 02142
www.oattravel.com

Paddling South Tours
PO Box 827
Calistoga, CA 94515
707-942-4550
tourbaja@aol.com

Preferred Adventures, Ltd.
1 West Water Street
St. Paul, MN 55107
651-222-8131
travel@preferredadventures.com

Raven Adventures
39 Glasheen Road
Petersham, MA 01366
978-724-3530
globalcr@crocker.com

Sea & Adventures
749 Trail Creek Road
Livingston, MT 59047
406-522-7595
sea@kayakbaja.com

Society Expeditions
2001 Western Ave., Suite 300
Seattle, WA 98121
206-728-94000
info@societyexpeditions.com

Southwind Adventures, Inc.
9900 W. Stanford Ave.
Littleton, CO 80123
303-972-0701
info@southwindadventures.com

Swallows and Amazons
Box 771
Eastham, MA 02642
508-255-1886

Tamu Safaris
PO Box 175
Brooksville, Maine 04617
404-256-4727
cosal@tamusafaris.com

TourTech International
17780 Fitch, Suite 180
Irvine, CA 92614
949-476-1912
tourtech@pacbell.net

The Travel Centre
Box TTN 356t
8425 NW 29th Street
Miami, FL 33122
868-623-5096
trvlcentre@wow.net

Tread Lightly
37 Juniper Meadow Road
Washington Depot, CT 06794
860-868-1710
patread@aol.com

Triple E Inc.
2312 NW Kearney St
Portland, OR 97210
503-223-2626
erica@triplee.com

Victor Emanuel Tours
PO Box 33008
Austin TX 78764
512-328-5221
info@ventbird.com

Virginia Eastern Shore Corporation
PO Box 40
Melfa, VA 23410
757-442-7180
ras@vashore.com

Visionary Voyages
16057 Tampa Palms Blvd., Suite 347
Tampa, FL 33647
813-991-5903
VisionaryVoyages@aol.com

Voyagers International
PO Box 915
Ithaca, NY 14851
607-273-4321
explore@voyagers.com

Wilderness Travel
1102 Ninth St.
Berkely, CA 94710
800-368-2794
info@wildernesstravel.com

Wildland Adventures
3516 NE 155th St.
Seattle, WA 98155
800-345-4453
kurt@wildland.com

Windjammer Barefoot Cruises
1759 Bay Road
Miami Beach, FL 33139
305-672-6453

Whitt's Alaskan Adventures
PO Box 114
Mile 131.5 Denali Highway
Cantwell, AK 99729
888-764-2662
whittsadventures@lycos.com

Yes Tourism, Ltd.
PO Box 25307
Miami FL 33102
868-660-5520
yestour@trinidad.net

Zegrahm Expeditions, Inc.
192 Nickerson Street, Suite 200
Seattle, WA 98109
206-285-4000
zoe@zeco.com

U.S. TOUR OPERATORS LIST
(Members of the National Tour Association)

4th Dimension Tours
7101 SW 99th Ave.
Miami, FL 33173
800-343-0020

AAA Auto Club South
1515 Westshore Blvd.
Tampa, FL 33607

AAA Nebraska
910 North 96th St.
Omaha, Neb. 68103
402-390-1000

AAA Travel Agency
2900 AAA Court
Bettendorf, IW 52722
800-373-9609

AFC Tours11772 Sorrento Valley
Rd., # 101
San Diego, CA 92121
858-481-8188

All Aboard America
230 S. Country Club Dr.
Mesa, AZ 85210
800-962-4728

Alternative ToursPO
Box 8492
Cherry Hill, NJ 08002
856-854-6396

American Ring Travel
28110 Ave. Stanford, Unit A
Valencia,CA 91355
661-294-9033

Americantours International
6053 W. Century Blvd
Los Angeles, CA 90045
310-641-9953

Badger Coaches
220 W. Beltline Highway
Madison WI 53713
608-255-1511

Brendan Tours
3751 Seminole Circle
Fairfield, CA 94533
800-421-8446

Capital Management Group
1440 Clearview Ave. Suite 104
Mesa, AZ 85208
800-289-6441

Columbia Crossroads Tours
4800 SW Macadam Ave., #255
Portland OR 97201
503-225-9995

Carolinas Tourism Network
306 Neighbors Drive
Midland, NC 28107

Carol Love's Tours
412 N 4th St
Youngwood, PA 15697

Collette Tours
162 Middle Street
Pawtucket, RI 02860

Colonial Pathways
PO Box 879
Chadd's Ford, PA 19317

Contiki U.S. Holdings
2300m E Katella Ave, Suite 450
Anaheim, CA 92806
714-935-0808

Come Along Tours
PO Box 69
Whites Creek, TN 37189
615-876-7266

Country Squires Tours
PO Box 937
Centerville, MA 02632
508-771-1423

Coustom Tours
PO Box 961
La Grande OR 97850
541-963-3239

Creative Tours Inc.
1318 N Pine Hills Rd.
Orlando, FL 32808
407-293-2224

Cruises and Tours Worldwide
2440 S. Brentwood Blvd, #105
St. Louis, MO 63144

Daphne's Tour and Travel
2412 Line Ave.
Amarillo, TX 79106
800-372-3535

Discovery Unlimited Tours
15061 Springdale St. Suite 210
Huntington Beach, CA 92649
714-895-1555

East Town Travel
765 N. Broadway
Milwaukee, WI 53202
414-276-3131

Especially 4-U
7440 E. Main Street, Suite 2-A
Mesa, AZ 85207
800-331-4968

Friendship Tours
533 Cottage Grove Road
Bloomfield, CT 06002
800-243-8836

Gala Tours International
21311 Hawthorne Blvd, Suite 200
Torrance, CA 90503
310-316-7355

Getaway Tours
P.O Box 70
Terryville, CT
800-247-5457

Go with Jo
910 Dixieland Road
Harlingen, TX 78552
956-43-1446

Gold Road Tours
2260 Bryce Lane
Lake Havasu City, AZ 86406
805-340-3821

Golden Age Festival
5501 New jersey Ave.
Wildwood Crest NJ 08260
609-522-3616

Great Southern Travel
1729 W. Highway 76
Branson, MO 65616
417-334-8069

Great Western Tours
3814 E. Colorado Blvd. Suite 200
Pasadena, CA 91107
626-578-1161

Gulf South Travel
11821 Coursey Blvd.
Baton Rouge, LA 70816
225-293-9586

Harmon Tours
PO Box 7727
Boise, ID 83707
800-627-1315

Hesselgrave International Tours
PO Box 30768
Bellingham, WA 98228
360-734-3570

Holland America Line
300 Elliot Ave. W.
Seattle, WA 98119
206-281-0566

Hyde's Encore Tours
2122 W. 5400 S.
Salt Lake City, UT 84118
801-966-4242

Julian Tours
624 N. Washington St.
Alexandria, VA 22314
703-684-9800

Lamers Tour and Travel
1126 W. Boden Court
Milwaukee, WI 53221
414-281-2002

Landmark Tours
208 College Highway, Suite 4
Southwick, MA 01077
413-569-1500

Main Street Tours
1751 W. Torrance Blvd. Suite N
Torrance, CA 90501
800-300-6246

Mark Bryars Travel
PO Box 590
Waycross, GA 31502
912-283-1314

Maupintour
1421 Research Park Dr., # 300
Lawrence, KS 66049
800-255-4266

McClures Tours and Travel
417 3rd Street
Marietta, GA 45750

Midwest Charter Tours
7601 S. Cicero, Suite 201
Chicago, IL 60652
773-585-0700

My World Travel
PO Box 7079
Wilmington, DL 19803
800-822-0922

Nationwide Travelers Tours
1103 Lynndale Dr.
Appleton, WI 54914
920-734-5620

PML Travel
525 Rte. 73 S.
Evesham Township, NJ 08053
609-983-1866

Palmetto Tours
813-B Bay Street
Myrtle Beach, SC 29577
843-626-2431

Passport Travel and Tours
PO Box 270
Mount Prospect, IL 60056
847-225-7050

Roamer Tours
PO Box 1299
Reading, PA 19603
610-376-6361

Seaway Destinations
707 Cayuga Creek Road
Buffalo, NY 14227
716-892-0482

Sports Liesure Vacations
9521-H Folsom Blvd,
Sacremento, CA 95827
800-951-5556

Teddy Bear Tours
PO Box10217
Seminole, FL 33773
727-397-6464

Tour Carriage Inc.
1243 S. 7th St., Suite B
Phoenix, AZ 85034
800-445-0628

Travel Fun Tours
PO Box 775
New Ulm, MN 56073
507-233-4000

Travel Organizers
7373 S. Alton Way, #B-100
Englewood, CO 80112
800-283-2754

Trips Travel
8535 North Dixie Drive
Dayton, OH 45414
800-500-1072

Turner Coaches Inc.
2135 E. Margaret Dr.
Terre Haute, IN 47802
800-873-5252

Tye's Top Tour and Travel
380 S W Highway, Suite 4
Merrimack, NH 03054
800-374-6819

USA Student Travel
5080 Robert J Mathews Pkwy.
El Dorado Hills, CA 95762
800-448-4444

US Gateways
553 Willow Ave.
Cedarhurst, NY 11516
516-374-4455

Vermont Transit
106 Main Street
Burlington VT 05401
800-642-3133

Viking Travel Service
140 N. La Grange Rd.
La Grange, IL 60525
708-482-3445

White Star Tours
26 E Lancaster Ave.
Reading, PA 19607
800-437-2323

Annex E

PUBLICATIONS AND REPORTS CONSULTED
ECOTOURISM BIBLIOGRAPHY

ARA Consulting Group and HLA Consultants (1994), Ecotourism – Nature/Adventure/Culture: Alberta and British Columbia Market Demand Assessment, (prepared for Canadian Heritage, Industry Canada, et. al., December 1994).

Eagles, Paul F. J. (1994), "Understanding the Market for Sustainable Tourism" in McCool, Stephen F.; Watson, Alan E. (comps.) Linking Tourism, the Environment, and Sustainability, Volume of compiled papers from a special session of the annual meeting of the National Parks and Recreation Association (available on The International Ecotourism Society Website www.ecotourism.org).

Eubanks, Ted (2001), "Sustainable Tourism in Natural Areas Market Study" (draft prepared for the Commission for Environmental Cooperation, Montreal, Quebec).

Filion, Fern L., James Foley, and Andre Jacquemont (1992), "The Economics of Global Ecotourism", unpublished report on file at: Canadian Wildlife Service, Environment Canada, Hull, PQ.

Frechtling, Douglas C. (1996), Practical Tourism Forecasting, (Butterworth-Heinmann, Oxford, England.

Hall, C. Michael and Alan Lew (eds.) (1998), Sustainable Tourism: A Geographical Perspective, (Addison Wesley Longman Ltd.).

Hawkins, Donald, Megan Epler Wood, and Sam Bittman (eds.) (1995), The Ecolodge Sourcebook: for Planners and Developers, (The Ecotourism Society).

Inskeep, Edward (1991), Tourism Planning: An Integrated and Sustainable Development Approach, (Van Nostrand Reinhold, N.Y.).

Lane, Bernard, (1999), "Sustainable Tourism in the Twenty-First Century, presentation to the International Institute for Peace Through Tourism Conference, Glascow, Scotland, October 20, 1999.

Leones, Julie, Bonnie Colby, and Kristine Crandall (1998), "Tracking Expenditures of the Elusive Nature Tourists of Southeastern Arizona", Journal of Travel Research, Winter, 1998.

Lindberg, Kreg (1991), Policies for Maximizing Nature Tourism's Ecological and Economic Benefits, (Washington, DC, World Resources Institute).

Lindberg, Kreg, and Donald Hawkins (eds.) (1993)Ecotourism: A Guide for Planners and Managers, (The Ecotourism Society).

Lindberg, Kreg, Megan Epler Wood, and David Engledrum 1(1998), The Ecolodge Sourcebook: A Guide for Planners and Managers, Volume 2, (The Ecotoursim Society).

Lindberg, Kreg and Jeremy Enriquez (no date), "An Analysis of Ecotourism's Economic Contribution to Conservation and Development in Belize, Volume 1: Summary Report"
(World Wildlife Fund).

MacGregor, James R., "Sustainable Tourism Development" in Encycopedia for Hospitality and Tourism (Van Nostrand-Rheinholt).

McKercher, Bob (1998), The Business of Nature Based Tourism, (Hospitality Press, Melbourne, Australia).

Meric, Havva, and Judith Hunt (1998), "Ecotourists' Motivational and Demographic Characteristics: A Case of North Carolina Travelers", Journal of Travel Research, Spring, 1998.

Orams, M. (1995), "Towards a More Desirable Form of Ecotourism", Tourism Management, (1995).

Outdoor Recreation Coalition of America (ORCA) (no date), "The Emerging Market for Outdoor Recreation in the United States: Based on the National Survey on Recreation and the Environment", (available on the ORCA Website at http://www.outdoorlink.com)

Palacio, Vincent and Stephen F. McCool (1997), "Identifying Ecotourists in Belize Through Benefit Segmentation: A Preliminary Analysis", Journal of Sustainable Tourism, Vol. 5, No.3, 1997

Saleh, Farouk and Judy Karwacki (1996), "Revisiting the Ecotourist: The Case of G rasslands National Park", Journal of Sustainable Tourism, Vol. 4, No. 2.

Sanders, Edward G. and Elizabeth Halpenny (2001), The Business of Ecolodges: The Economics and Financing of Ecolodges, (The International Ecotourism Society, Burlington, VT).

Sinclair, M. Thea and Mike Stabler (1997), The Economics of Tourism, (Routledge, London & New York).

Stabler, Michael J. (199_), Tourism and Sustainability, (CABI _____)

Sweeting, James E. N., et. al. (1999), The Green Host Effect: An Integrated Approach to Sustainable Tourism and Resort Development, (Conservation International, Washington D.C.)

Travel Industry Publishing (2001), Travel Industry World 2000 Yearbook: The Big Picture, (Travel Industry Publishing Company, Inc., New York).

Tourism Development Authority of Egypt (1999), Guidelines for Eco-Lodge Development, (TDA, Cairo, Egypt)

Urban Land Institute (1997), Resort Development Handbook, (ULI, Washington D.C.)

WTTC - World Travel and Tourism Council (1992), "Travel and Tourism in the World Economy", (Brussels, Belgium).

WTO – World Tourism Organization, Yearbook of Tourism Statistics (2001), (WTO, Madrid, Spain).

Walsh, Richard G. (1986), Recreation Economic Decisions: Comparing Benefits and Costs, (Venture Publishing, Inc., State College Pennsylvania).

Weaver, David B. (1999), "Magnitude of Ecotourism in Costa Rica and Kenya", Annals of Tourism Research, (October, 1999).

Weiler, Betty and Tracey Johnson (1991), "Nature Based Tour Operators: Are They Environmentally Friendly or are the Faking It?", Proceedings of a National Tourism Research Council, (Institute of Industrial Economics, University of New Castle, Australia).

Wellner, Alison S. (1997), Americans at Play: Demographics of Outdoor Recreation & Travel, (New Strategies Publications, Inc., Ithaca, New York).

Wight, Pamela A. (1995), "North American Ecotourists: Market Profile and Trip Characteristics" (available on The Ecotourism Society Website, www.ecotourism.org)

Wight, Pamela A. (1996a), "North Amercian Ecotourists: Market Profile and Trip Characteristics", Journal of Travel Research, Spring, 1996.

Wight, Pamela A. (1996b), "North American Ecotourism Markets: Motivations, Preferences, and Destinations", Journal of Travel Research, Summer, 1996, (also available on The International Ecotourism Society Website, www.ecotourism.org).

Wight, Pamela A. (1998), "Tools for Sustainability Analysis in Planning and Managing Tourism and Recreation in the Destination" in Hall, C. Michael and Alan Lew (eds) Sustainable Tourism: A Geographical Perspective, (Addison Wesley Longman Ltd.)

Wight, Pamela A. (1999), "Catalogue of Exemplary Practices in Adventure Travel and Tourism", (Prepared by Pam Wight and Associates on behalf of the Canadian Tourism Commission, March ,1999).

Weaver, David B. (1999), "Magnitude of Ecotourism in Costa Rica and Kenya", Journal of Travel Research, 1999.